THE COMPLETE SLOW COOKING FOR TWO

THE COMPLETE
SLOW COOKING
FOR TWO

A PERFECTLY PORTIONED
SLOW COOKER COOKBOOK

LINDA LARSEN

SONOMA
PRESS

Sonoma Press publishes its books in a variety of electronic and print formats. Some content that appears in print may not be available in electronic books, and vice versa.

TRADEMARKS: Sonoma Press and the Sonoma Press logo are trademarks or registered trademarks of Callisto Media Inc. and/or its affiliates, in the United States and other countries, and may not be used without written permission. All other trademarks are the property of their respective owners. Sonoma Press is not associated with any product or vendor mentioned in this book.

Photography © Offset/Johnny Autry, front cover and p.64; Stockfood/George Blomfield, p.2; Stocksy/Trinette Reed, p.7; Stockfood/Sporrer/Skowronek, p.8; Stockfood/Emel Ernalbant, p.24; Stockfood/Fotos mit Geschmack, p.34; Stockfood/Wissing, Michael, p.43; Stockfood/Sporrer/Skowronek, p.46; Stocksy/Davide Illini, p.52; Stockfood/Morgans, Gareth, p.59; Stockfood/Morgans, Gareth, p.72; Stockfood/Gräfe & Unzer Verlag /Schardt, Wolfgang, p.78; Stockfood/Condé Nast Collection, p.85; Stockfood/Snowflake Studios Inc., p.92; Stockfood/Leigh Beisch, p.100; Stockfood/Leigh Beisch, p.108; Stockfood/Keller & Keller Photography, p.119; Stockfood/Shea Evans, p.126; Stockfood/Gareth Morgans, p.130; Stockfood/Keller & Keller Photography, p.136; Stockfood/Tina Rupp, p.142; Stockfood/Valérie Lhomme, p.148; Stockfood/Jonathan Gregson, p.157; Stockfood/Shea Evans, p.166; Stockfood/Gareth Morgans, p.170; Stockfood/Maja Smend, p.178; Stocksy/Harald Walker, p.187; Stockfood/People Pictures, p.192; Stockfood/Renée Comet, p.200; Stockfood/Samantha Linsell, p.207; Stockfood/Stacy Ventura, p.212; Stockfood/Joanne Schmaltz, p.220; Stockfood/Danny Lerner, p.227; Stockfood/Food Experts Group, p.230; Stockfood/Gareth Morgans, p.238; Stocksy/Harald Walker, p.248; Stocksy/Marta Muñoz-Calero Calderon, p.250

ISBN: Print 978-1-942411-19-2 | eBook 978-1-942411-20-8

Contents

JUST THE TWO OF US

When I first got married, I cooked the way my mother did: using the stove top and oven—that is, *when* I cooked. Finding it difficult to face the kitchen after a long day of work, my husband and I often went out to eat or relied on frozen pizza. I certainly did not have a slow cooker; by the 1980s, they were already considered archaic and cumbersome.

Soon after the Rival company introduced the first slow cooker, called the Crock-Pot, in 1971, most slow-cooker recipes consisted of some type of meat, cream of "something" soup, and a few vegetables that cooked into a hearty, but boring "hot dish." It was such a novelty to throw food into an appliance, turn it on, leave the house, and come home to a finished dinner. Working mothers in particular embraced this new trend. Since the slow-cooker recipes at the time focused more on convenience than taste, it wasn't long before the complaints started to trickle in. Many thought the food was underflavored, that everything that came out of it looked the same, or that the recipes relied too much on canned and processed foods. By the early 1980s, interest in the slow cooker had waned.

About fifteen years ago, new versions of the slow cooker started appearing on the market. I began taking notice when, at the store, I saw a beautiful slow cooker made of stainless steel. It was nothing like the ugly avocado-green slow cookers I had seen before. Chefs started inventing slow-cooker recipes that made the slow cooker's old reputation recede—recipes like Cuban black beans and rice, French cassoulet, or spicy tamales. A slowing economy and more women in the workforce meant more people were looking for ways to prepare delicious food quickly that would still fit within the family budget. The slow cooker seemed the ideal solution.

And so I ventured into the slow-cooking world and never looked back. Most people know that slow cookers are ideal appliances for making big batches of food. But, depending on the size you buy, slow cookers can also be perfect for making meals for two. It has always been just my husband and myself for our whole married life. The slow cooker makes cooking so simple, and portion control is automatic. I use the slow cooker a few times a week, all year round, for

everything from stews to sandwich fillings to desserts and breakfasts. Slow cooking is so much easier and healthier than cooking a microwave dinner or going to a drive-through for some fast food, and the food that comes out of this appliance is delicious, well flavored, complex, and interesting. One of the best benefits of the slow cooker is the aroma when you open the front door!

In this book you will learn why the slow cooker is such a great choice for two people, how to choose a slow cooker, and how to use it to its maximum potential. You'll find tips for shopping along with tricks for using common kitchen tools to make the slow-cooker experience even better. Most of the recipes in this book are one-pot recipes. That means you put food in the slow cooker, turn it on, and go about your day. The recipes in this book will fit many dietary restrictions and can be changed to suit your tastes and budget. Preparation time will be less than twenty minutes for each recipe. After eight hours of simmering (but no work on your part), you'll sit down to a delicious dinner. Let's cook!

ONE

SLOW COOKING

DESIGNED FOR DUOS

Despite—and in many cases because of—the many technological advances that work to make our lives easier and more fun, we seem to have less time than ever before. When we're not in the office, at school, or fitting in a little bit of time for hobbies, our minutes seem to be dominated by devices, whether we're checking e-mail, playing games, or streaming one television show after the next. Trying to create additional time for healthy, flavorful meals that don't create another problem— tons of leftovers and days upon days of eating the same meals—can feel impossible. That's where slow cooking comes in. This old-school appliance, getting ever more modern and popular each year, doesn't judge you for where and how you want to spend your time. It simply accepts the burden of doing your cooking for you.

A wonderful shortcut that feels like cheating, slow cooking offers a great way to cook for two. Whether you and your roommate have different schedules or you and your spouse work different shifts, everyone can come home to a delicious, nutritious, home-cooked meal that's ready to eat. Plus, slow cooking is a money saver. It turns those tough, less expensive cuts of meat into melt-in-your-mouth revelations after long cooking in a low, moist heat. If meat is not your thing, you can make plenty of other dishes in your slow cooker—from breakfast to beans to casseroles and more.

Slow cooking recipes have come a long way since the introduction of the appliance. Gone are the bland recipes that use minimal herbs and spices and end up looking just about as appetizing as the plate they're on. With this cookbook, you can choose to have Jambalaya (page 141), Red Curry Beef (page 97), or Carnitas (page 93) any night of the week without dealing with unused ingredients or portions.

WHY SLOW COOK?

Slow cookers are unique appliances, different from a stand-alone roaster or steamer. Here are a handful of reasons slow cooking just makes sense:

IT'S HEALTHIER THAN OTHER COOKING METHODS. Slow cooking is a healthy way to cook food. The low temperatures cook food safely but slowly, preserving valuable nutrients. When foods are cooked at high heat, harmful compounds such as advanced glycation end products (AGEs) form. AGEs contribute to insulin resistance and inflammation. The slow cooker completely eliminates this risk. Also, using fresh foods and avoiding highly processed ingredients is a much healthier choice than other time-saving alternatives such as prepackaged meals and frozen dinners.

IT FREES UP TIME. You'll save lots of time in the kitchen when you use a slow cooker. Most of these recipes involve just a few preparation steps; then you combine everything in the appliance and turn it on.

IT SAVES YOU MONEY. You can use much less expensive cuts of meat in the slow cooker. Expensive beef cuts such as filet mignon do not cook well in low, moist heat. Cuts such as chuck and round are perfect for the slow cooker's self-basting mechanism. Less expensive chicken thighs also cook to tender perfection in the slow cooker. Cheaper root vegetables such as turnips, potatoes, and carrots are also ideal ingredients for this cooking method.

THE RESULTS ARE DELICIOUS. Meat becomes incredibly tender in this appliance. Connective tissue and gelatin break down in beef, pork, lamb, and poultry when cooked in the slow cooker, and fat melts and spreads through the cut. Vegetables, especially hard root vegetables, become fork tender and very sweet. Grains, including oatmeal, farro, wild rice, and barley, cook to nutty and tender perfection. You can even make amazing desserts, from rich puddings to decadent cakes.

IT'S AN ECO-FRIENDLY WAY TO COOK. Your slow cooker is a great energy saver. It will not heat up the kitchen in the summer and put a strain on your air conditioner. A slow cooker will use about 125 watts per hour on low. That works out to about 1.5 cents per hour in an area that charges 12 cents per kilowatt hour. The average oven costs about 10 cents per kilowatt hour, so even with a shorter cooking time, using your oven costs more.

IT TAKES TWO

We are: Cati, 35, and Megan, 34

Cooking together since: 2006

How we met: We bonded in our first year of graduate school over our mutual love of cats, queso, and Canadian teen dramas, and became roommates—and platonic life partners!—shortly thereafter.

The foods we love: breakfast tacos, pizza, sushi, chips, and the aforementioned queso. Do Bloody Marys count as a food?

How we cook: As roommates, we grocery shopped together, taking turns buying and sharing the staples, then buying our own favorites separately. Since Megan's a vegetarian and I am not, we couldn't pool our grocery bill completely. I was always more of the daily cook, but Megan had some specialties she would often serve up, including a very tasty tofu stir-fry. When we had dinner parties, I handled menu planning, but we'd shop and cook together. We were kind of famous within our circle for hosting elaborate theme parties with tons of great food, signature cocktails, and outsized budgets for our meager grad student stipends. Once we spent over $500 on a haunted birthday party. But damn, that witches' brew and the red velvet cake with black icing were worth it!

HOW THE SLOW COOKER WORKS

A true slow cooker consists of a thin round or oval metal surround encasing a metal or ceramic insert. A glass or plastic lid fits snugly onto the insert. Heating coils in the surround heat up and evenly heat the insert, which then transfers heat to the food.

TEMPERATURE

Most slow cookers come with three settings: keep warm, low, and high. The keep-warm temperature is about 160°F, just above the lowest safe temperature (140°F) for holding food. Low is about 200°F, and high is about 300°F. Most of the recipes in this book use the low setting so that you can cook for at least seven hours, giving you an entire day, or night, to walk away from the slow cooker. The general rule of thumb is that one hour on high is equal to two hours on low.

STEAM COOKING

Because the lid fits snugly, steam gets trapped in the slow cooker as the food heats up. This "wet" cooking method cooks gently and thoroughly. The steam also creates a slight vacuum seal between the lid and the insert, which keeps volatile nutrients such as vitamins B and C in the slow cooker while locking in flavor compounds. Wet cooking methods are excellent with tougher cuts of meat, soups, stews, casseroles, and side dishes.

FIVE SLOW COOKER MYTHS (AND WHY THEY'RE WRONG)

SLOW COOKED FOODS ARE BLAND. Long, slow cooking using wet heat can mute the flavors of herbs, but that is easily fixed by adding more of the herbs just before serving. Slow cooked foods are actually more flavorful than foods cooked on the stove top, since there is no evaporation of volatile compounds.

SLOW COOKERS ARE ONLY GOOD FOR SOUPS, STEWS, AND CHILIS. Your slow cooker can make lasagna, mashed potatoes, beans, grains, breakfast cereals, bread puddings, and even cheesecakes.

SLOW COOKERS OVERCOOK VEGETABLES. The key to cooking perfectly tender vegetables is layering. Tough root vegetables should be prepped into even cuts and placed at the bottom. More tender veggies such as corn and peas should be at the top.

SLOW COOKED FOOD IS WATERY AND THIN. Do not add more liquid to your slow cooker than the recipe specifies. There is no evaporation during cooking, and the ingredients give off liquid as they cook.

SLOW COOKERS DO NOT COOK FOOD EVENLY. Again, layering is important for even cooking. Tough vegetables belong at the bottom, followed by meats, then tender vegetables on top. And make sure vegetables and fruits with the same texture are cut to the same size so they cook evenly.

IT TAKES TWO

We are: Min, 32, and Tim, 36
www.mjandhungryman.com

Cooking together since: 2006

How we met: Although our families had known each other for years, it took a fortuitous, post-college Thanksgiving reunion to bring us together.

The foods we love: Korean BBQ, roasted sweet potatoes, wood-fired pizza, quinoa, salmon.

How we cook: Being in the kitchen together is kind of our escape from the daily grind, starting with the shopping. On the weekends, we love strolling the aisles of the grocery store or our local farmers' market and allowing in-season ingredients to inspire our menus, but we make sure to take along a list as well to keep us on track. Although Tim was definitely savvier with the cooking early on in our relationship, he now recognizes that the kitchen is my playground. I do most of the work, from prepping to doing the dishes, but when there's shellfish or meat to be cleaned, Tim will gladly come to my aid. Also, I leave all the grilling to him because he just seems to have a knack for it. Tim is best with casseroles, lasagnas, and pretty much anything else you can throw in a pan and bake. As a registered dietitian, I enjoy putting twists on classic dishes by ramping up their nutrition content with real, wholesome foods. I'm also a huge fan of my slow cooker. Two of my signature recipes are made in the slow cooker: Korean Spicy Chicken and Potatoes and Tex-Mex Beef Fajitas.

THE RIGHT COOKER FOR TWO

Choosing your slow cooker is a matter of personal preference. You can buy a stainless steel cooker or one with a colorful pattern to match your kitchen.

SIZE

You may already own a slow cooker that you want to use today, but the size of the slow cooker must be appropriate for the recipe amounts. To cook safely, slow cookers must be filled one-half to three-quarters full.

Because the recipes in this book are made to serve two people, the best sizes of slow cooker are also the most common: 3- or 3½-quart slow cookers. You can find them in most big-box stores as well as online. These slow cookers will hold about 7 to 9 cups of food to serve two people generously, with the possibility of leftovers for lunch the next day. So if you make lasagna in a slow cooker this size, you can enjoy it for dinner and have enough left over for a ready-made lunch the next day—but you won't be stuck eating it the entire week. None of these recipes will require making space in your freezer, except for broths and sauces made in bulk, and side dishes.

FEATURES

Slow cookers come with a wide variety of features ranging from different shapes and patterns to transportability (great if you're doing a potluck) to programmable timing.

You'll find that most 3-quart slow cookers on the market these days are round while the 3½-quart models are rectangular, oval, or round. They are available in fun patterns and colors from flowers to tiger stripes and stainless to magenta.

Make sure your slow cooker has a removable insert for easier cleaning. Luckily, most of the slow cookers on the market today have this feature.

Slow cookers still have two temperatures—the low-heat setting and the high-heat setting—but the keep-warm feature is relatively new. The ability to program cooking time is very valuable if you are gone for more than eight hours during the day. With this feature, once the slow cooker gets to the end of the cook time, it doesn't just turn off but switches over to the keep-warm setting for two hours. Don't forget that new slow cookers cook at hotter temperatures than those made ten years ago. Back then the low setting was 180°F (today it's about 200°F), and the high setting was 230°F (today it's about 300°F). So if you are using an older slow cooker, you may need to increase the time the food cooks when you make these recipes.

SLOW COOKER OR CROCK-POT
WHAT'S THE DIFFERENCE?

Slow cooker is the generic name for an appliance that has heating elements all around the insert that quickly bring food up to safe temperatures. *Crock-Pot* is the Rival corporation's registered trademark for its slow cookers. All Crock-Pots are slow cookers, but not all slow cookers are Crock-Pots. Other popular slow cooker brands include All-Clad, Cuisinart, and Hamilton Beach.

When you're shopping, keep in mind that there are appliances on the market referred to as slow cookers that have their heating element only on the bottom. Don't buy one of these to use for the recipes in this book. Appliances with heating elements only on the bottom heat food more slowly. Experts do not recommend cooking large cuts of meat in this type of slow cooker (although it works for soups and stews). When purchasing your slow cooker, make sure it is a true one—with heating elements all around the insert.

BRAND

Slow cookers, you will find, are a relatively inexpensive investment with many brands to choose from. The most popular brand, **Crock-Pot**, is made by Rival. Their 3-quart color slow cooker and stainless steel slow cooker sell for about $20. The 3½-quart model is available for about $40 in a rectangular shape, which is perfect for making dishes such as lasagna. Rival also makes a 3½-quart oval slow cooker that will hook up to other slow cookers for buffet serving. Those are more expensive, at around $50.

Hamilton Beach makes a lot of pretty 3-quart slow cookers that come with a metal surround in different colors and patterns. The prices for these slow cookers range from $25 to $40, depending on the pattern. The slow cookers have keep-warm, low, and high settings.

Cuisinart has a programmable 3½-quart slow cooker that makes slow cooking about as easy as you can possibly imagine. The oval shape and stainless steel surround are very attractive, and the cooker has keep-warm, simmer, low, and high settings. It sells for about $60. (Note that these prices were accurate at the time of writing and are subject to change.)

USING YOUR SLOW COOKER: DOS & DON'TS

There are some rules you must follow when using a slow cooker, both for safety and to ensure the finished result will be delicious.

DO:

SPRAY THE INSERT WITH NONSTICK COOKING SPRAY BEFORE ADDING FOOD. The food will not stick to the insert, and cleanup will be much easier.

THINK ABOUT SAUTÉING AROMATICS SUCH AS ONIONS AND GARLIC BEFORE YOU ADD THEM TO THE SLOW COOKER. Doing so helps the flavor develop, and these vegetables will become sweet and tender.

THAW FROZEN FOODS BEFORE ADDING THEM TO THE SLOW COOKER. Frozen foods may stay in the danger zone of 40°F to 140°F too long and will reduce the temperature of other foods as they cook. Very large frozen foods, such as pot roast, may not cook through in the allotted time. Thaw these foods overnight in the refrigerator—never on the counter.

CUT THE SAME DENSITIES OF FOOD INTO THE SAME SIZE PIECES. Carrots, potatoes, onions, and sweet potatoes should be the same size so they cook evenly and at the same time.

USE WOODEN, PLASTIC, OR NONSTICK UTENSILS WHEN STIRRING OR SERVING FOOD. Metal tools can scratch the ceramic insert, causing liquid to seep out and the insert to eventually crack.

DON'T:

LIFT THE LID TO CHECK ON THE FOOD AS THE SLOW COOKER IS COOKING. Every time you lift the lid, the steam and slight vacuum seal between the lid and insert is released, dropping the temperature and lengthening the cooking time.

ADD TOO MUCH LIQUID. There is little to no evaporation in a slow cooker. Adding more liquid than the recipe calls for will result in watery food and decreased flavor.

STORE FOOD IN THE INSERT. The insert is made for holding heat. If you store hot food in the insert and put it in the refrigerator, the food will take too long to cool to a safe temperature and bacteria may grow.

ADD GROUND MEATS WITHOUT PRECOOKING THEM. Ground meats will become mushy and fatty if put in the slow cooker uncooked, adding too much fat to the recipe.

ADD INGREDIENTS SUCH AS PASTA, SHRIMP, TENDER VEGETABLES, OR DAIRY BEFORE THE LAST 30 MINUTES OF COOKING TIME. Pasta, shrimp, and tender veggies can easily overcook, and dairy will curdle if heated too long.

CONVERTING A STOVE-TOP RECIPE TO THE SLOW COOKER

One of the best things about the slow cooker is that you can take a stove-top recipe and adjust a few details to make it work in the appliance. Soups, chilis, stews, roasts, and meat with vegetables are all perfect for conversion. Keep these principles in mind.

> **Decrease the amount of liquid called for by about half.** But keep in mind this caveat: For any recipe that cooks rice, pasta, or beans, you must have twice as much liquid as ingredient by weight to cook properly, since they absorb water as they cook. So, for example, a recipe that uses one cup of rice should have at least two cups of liquid.

> **Trim excess fat from meats and poultry.** Too much fat in a slow cooker will raise the temperature, and the food may overcook. Plus, excess fat will make the food unpleasantly greasy.

> **Put veggies in the bottom and meats on top for even cooking.** Although everything cooks together in a saucepan or pot on the stove, proper layering is essential to avoid overcooking vegetables in the slow cooker.

In general, 1 hour of simmering on the stove top is equal to 6 to 8 hours on low in the slow cooker. A recipe that simmers for 30 minutes would cook in 4 to 6 hours on low in the slow cooker.

FOIL TO THE RESCUE

You definitely want to have heavy-duty aluminum foil on hand if you plan to use your slow cooker often. Foil is a versatile tool with many uses.

> **Make slings out of the foil to put under meatloaf or lasagna so you can lift the finished product right out of the appliance.** Tear off a 24-inch piece of heavy-duty foil, and fold it in half lengthwise two or three times. Place it in the slow cooker. Repeat with a second piece of foil, and then place this piece in the slow cooker so the foil crosses, making an "X" at the bottom.

> **Line the slow cooker with foil for super-easy cleanup and to shield the edges to prevent overcooking or burning.** Pasta dishes and casseroles do well with a foil liner.

> **Layer vegetables, meat, seasonings, and a bit of liquid on a piece of heavy-duty foil to make individual one-dish meals.** Close the packets and place them in the slow cooker.

> **Ball up pieces of aluminum foil to roast a chicken in the slow cooker.** The extra height acts like a rack, keeping the bird out of the rendered liquid so that it roasts instead of braises.

SHOPPING FOR MEALS

Shopping for two can sometimes feel like a juggling act. You need to limit the amount you buy so you don't waste food, but packages are often geared toward large families. Your hands aren't entirely tied, however. With a few targeted tips, you'll have no problem keeping any waste to a minimum.

PANTRY ITEMS

Purchase foods that keep well in the pantry in bulk, and make sure you compare the price per ounce of different-size packages. For instance, if you cook with dried beans often, a 5-pound bag, which will last for at least a year, is a better buy than a 16-ounce bag. Canned foods will last for years and should be consistently replenished. When it comes to dried spices, however, buy small bottles, as these lose their strength after a year.

FRESH PRODUCE, MEAT, AND HERBS

If possible, purchase the fresh foods that you store in the refrigerator a few times a week so that your recipes use the freshest possible ingredients. Planning your menu weekly helps decrease the chance of any food going to waste. During your planning, determine whether you can use ingredients more than once. For instance, if you need ¼ cup of chopped bell pepper for one recipe, pick another recipe that will use the rest of the vegetable later in the week. Be sure to store cut produce in plastic bags so they don't wilt or dry out. You can also add any leftover vegetables to other recipes, even if they aren't called for. For example, chopped zucchini would be a great addition to chicken soup or even chili, and leftover green beans would be delicious added to a pot roast.

Animal Protein

Make sure you carefully check expiration dates on meat, seafood, and poultry so you know you're preparing food that is safe to eat. Don't buy more meat than a recipe calls for unless you are prepared to repackage and freeze some of it.

IT TAKES TWO

We are: Susy, 62, and Louie, 61

Cooking together since: 1975

How we met: At the University of San Francisco, where we both went to college.

The foods we love: Our family's own Secret Spaghetti Sauce (a recipe handed down from Louie's Aunt Dolly), anything barbecued or grilled (especially chicken and lamb), slow-cooked Carne Adovada made with red chile pods from New Mexico, and stir-fries with lots of vegetables and greens from the farmers' market.

How we cook: We usually sit down together on Saturday morning and make a menu plan and shopping list for the coming week. We try to work in at least one dinner recipe we haven't made before. We trade off on who does the cooking, depending on who's home in time, though there are some things Louie likes to cook (the aforementioned Sauce, barbecue) and Susy does all the baking.

Fresh Produce

Purchase just enough tender produce, like bell peppers or tomatoes, for a specific recipe. This is where menu planning goes a long way toward helping you buy just what you need, and no more. Hardier fare, like onions, potatoes, sweet potatoes, and garlic, can be purchased in larger quantities, but be careful how you store them. Onions and potatoes should be stored away from each other, since keeping them in proximity can cause the other to spoil rapidly.

Herbs

Purchase fresh herbs in small quantities as well. To keep them fresh longer, cut off the ends and store them upright in a small glass of water in the fridge. To store fresh herbs longer, chop them up, place in a small container in 1-tablespoon amounts, and freeze. Frozen herbs can be added directly to the slow cooker without thawing first.

THE BIRD, THE COW, THE PIG, AND THE POT

What part of the animal gets you the tastiest dinner?

The chicken parts to use are bone-in chicken breasts and boneless thighs. With the breasts, the bone slows down the chicken's rate of cooking and adds lots of flavor to the entire dish. A bone-in chicken breast will cook in 6 to 7 hours, while a boneless one cooks in 4 to 5 hours. Don't forget to remove the skin—it becomes flabby with this cooking method—and don't brown the chicken before cooking unless the recipe calls for it.

The best beef cuts for the slow cooker include chuck eye roast, flank steak, bottom round, brisket, and short ribs. These inexpensive cuts become very tender when cooked in moist heat at low temperatures. Be sure to trim off excess fat before cooking these cuts. You can brown them before cooking in the slow cooker to add flavor, but that step isn't necessary, with the exception of ground beef, which must be browned and drained before use in slow-cooker recipes.

All types of pork work well in the slow cooker, from boneless chops to loin roasts. Chops become meltingly tender, while a pork shoulder can be shredded into a tender tangle that is perfect for sandwiches. Again, remember to trim and discard excess fat from pork cuts.

IT TAKES TWO

We are: Tim, 50, and Rebecca, 49

Cooking together since: 1990—if the boxed mac-n-cheese we made in our early days can be considered cooking.

How we met: In college as undergrads.

The foods we love: Lamb, duck, polenta, mushrooms, and risotto.

How we cook: Let's be honest here. Tim does 95 percent of the shopping and cooking, and I take care of the cleanup. We've tried cooking together but have found over the years that, for us, eating together is the real pleasure. As part-time residents of Napa Valley we have fallen in love with some of the region's small wineries. When we are in our East Coast home and begin to miss Northern California, we pick out a wine and plan a meal around it—cheaper than airfare!

RECIPES IN THIS BOOK

All the recipes are scaled to serve two people generously. As touched on before, some main dishes will give you enough food for leftovers for one or two people to enjoy the next day, but none are so large you'll need to worry about making space in your freezer. The recipes include many choices from cuisines around the world and range from simple broths and stocks to richly flavored lasagnas and casseroles.

You'll find that most of the recipes in the book (about three-quarters) are one-pot meals, meaning all you have to do is put all the ingredients in the insert at once and cook. The remaining dishes include a few extra steps, like limited use of the microwave, a sauté pan, or the food processor. Some foods, such as ground meat, must be cooked before going in the slow cooker, and other foods, such as stew meat, acquire deeper flavors if browned before being slow cooked. You can skip steps such as browning whole cuts of meat to save time, but the finished dish will not be as flavorful as it could be.

I've chosen recipes that make use of fresh foods and foods that don't contain lots of added sugar, preservatives, salt, or chemicals. The quality of your meal depends on the quality of the ingredients. Never cook with wilted vegetables, meats past their expiration date, or old spices.

If you have specific dietary restrictions, you'll find many recipes that either fit your restriction or are easily adaptable. For example, if a recipe calls for nuts, simply leave them out. You can substitute almond or rice flours for wheat flour. Recipes bear the labels vegan/vegetarian, gluten-free, soy-free, and/or nut-free to help you.

To make the most of every meal, I've included tips with many of the recipes. There are "Seasonal Substitution" tips, expert "Prep It Right" tips, and "Did You Know?" tips for ingredient information. "Perfect Pair" tips help you pull a meal together with little effort, and "Next Day" tips show how to transform any leftovers into another meal.

IT TAKES TWO

We are: Matt, 32, and Melissa, 31

Cooking together since: 2008, the year we started dating.

How we met: As freshmen in college.

The foods we love: Ramen, sushi, lasagna, tapas.

How we cook: For most of our relationship, I did most of the cooking. But after we got married, Matt took a basic knife skills class at a local cooking school and we subscribed to a meal subscription service—and that completely changed everything. The pre-portioned ingredients, easy-to-follow instructions, and introduction to new dishes really inspired Matt to get in the kitchen and try out cooking on his own. Now we enjoy cooking together, divvying up responsibilities (I am admittedly terrible with dishes), and surprising and delighting ourselves with what we're able to make with our own hands. We now want to start using our slow cooker (a wedding present, of course) more often to make meal prep even easier and healthier.

RUB A DUB DUB

Making your own spice rubs means you can customize them to your personal taste. Add them to pot roasts, meatloaf, and casseroles. To make the rubs, all you need are the right ingredients and a small bowl. Just put all the measured ingredients in and mix until they're well blended.

Keep these rubs in small glass jars with tight-fitting lids, and make sure to mark them with the recipe name and the date you made them. Store in a dark, cool, dry place.

CURRY RUB

Fragrant and spicy, this rub is perfect with chicken, beef, pork, or seafood. Adjust the ingredient amounts as you see fit to match your personal tastes. **Makes ¼ cup**

2 teaspoons ground turmeric
2 teaspoons curry powder
2 teaspoons ground ginger
1 teaspoon ground coriander
2 teaspoons salt
1 teaspoon ground paprika
1 teaspoon garlic powder
½ teaspoon ground cinnamon
½ teaspoon ground white pepper

ALL-AMERICAN DRY RUB

Sweet, spicy, and peppery, this rub is excellent added to pot roasts and meatloaf. **Makes ⅓ cup**

2 tablespoons brown sugar
1 tablespoon granulated sugar
1 teaspoon ground smoked paprika
1 teaspoon ground paprika
2 teaspoons salt
1 teaspoon freshly ground black pepper
1 teaspoon onion powder
1 teaspoon dried thyme leaves
¼ teaspoon ground mustard

JERK RUB

Aromatic spices come together with a hint of sweetness and a spicy kick, making this rub a go-to for grilled chicken and meats and a delicious addition to soups and casseroles.
Makes 3 tablespoons

2 teaspoons ground smoked paprika
2 teaspoons curry powder
1 teaspoon granulated sugar
1 teaspoon salt
1 teaspoon dried thyme leaves
½ teaspoon ground cayenne pepper
½ teaspoon crushed red pepper flakes
½ teaspoon ground cinnamon
¼ teaspoon ground allspice
¼ teaspoon freshly ground black pepper

TWO

BROTHS, SAUCES & CONDIMENTS

Broths, sauces, and condiments made in a slow cooker are far superior to their boxed, canned, and jarred brethren. Try making one of the tantalizing soups or chilis in chapter 3 using a broth or stock from this chapter as a base, or top your favorite taco or tortilla chips with one of the salsas found here. You won't regret taking the few minutes to make something that could never be mistaken for store-bought.

VEGETABLE BROTH

PREP
10 MINUTES

COOK
6 HOURS
ON LOW

GLUTEN-FREE

SOY-FREE

NUT-FREE

VEGAN

MAKES 8 CUPS

Not only is making your own broth a time and money saver, it's also good for you. Many canned broths have a lot of sodium, preservatives, colorings, and other chemicals you probably don't want to ingest—plus, they just aren't as flavor-rich as homemade ones. This broth, satisfying yet delicately flavored, is the perfect base for vegetable and vegan or vegetarian soups.

1 onion, chopped

2 celery stalks, chopped

¼ cup chopped celery leaves

1 garlic clove, sliced

1 large tomato, chopped

1 cup chopped cremini mushrooms

1 bay leaf

1 teaspoon dried thyme leaves

¼ teaspoon salt

4 peppercorns

6 cups cool water

1. In the slow cooker, combine the onion, celery, celery leaves, garlic, tomato, mushrooms, bay leaf, thyme, salt, and peppercorns; then add the water.

2. Cover and cook on low for 6 hours.

3. Strain into a large bowl, pressing on the ingredients to get all the liquid.

4. Use immediately, cover and refrigerate for up to 4 days, or freeze for up to 4 months.

PER SERVING (1 cup) Calories: 15; Total fat: 0g; Saturated fat: 0g; Cholesterol: 0mg; Carbohydrates: 3g; Fiber: 1g; Protein: 1g

PREP IT RIGHT Because this is a light broth, it tastes best when made with filtered water.

PREP
20 MINUTES

COOK
7 HOURS
ON LOW

GLUTEN-FREE

SOY-FREE

NUT-FREE

CHICKEN STOCK

MAKES 8 CUPS

Once you get a taste of this stock, you'll never purchase another can or box again. The rich, concentrated flavor adds depth to a myriad of recipes from the simple, like chicken soup, to the more complex, like curries and casseroles. Wondering why this is a stock and not a broth? The term *stock* applies when bones are used in the preparation.

1 pound chicken wings and bone-in thighs

1 onion, unpeeled and sliced

1 carrot, cut into chunks

2 celery stalks with leaves, chopped

2 garlic cloves, unpeeled, halved

2 tablespoons coarsely chopped fresh flat-leaf parsley

2 teaspoons fresh thyme leaves

1 teaspoon salt

¼ teaspoon freshly ground black pepper

6 cups cool water

1. In the slow cooker, combine the chicken, onion, carrot, celery with leaves, garlic, parsley, thyme, salt, and pepper; then add the water.

2. Cover and cook on low for 6 to 7 hours, or until the liquid is light gold.

3. Strain into a large bowl, pressing on the chicken and vegetables to get all the liquid.

4. Refrigerate the stock overnight; then remove and discard the layer of fat that accumulated on top.

5. Use immediately, refrigerate the stock for up to 4 days, or freeze in 1-cup portions for up to 4 months.

PER SERVING (1 cup) Calories: 85; Total fat: 3g; Saturated fat: 1g; Cholesterol: 7mg; Carbohydrates: 8g; Fiber: 0g; Protein: 6g

DID YOU KNOW? Roasting the chicken parts and onion before combining all the ingredients in the slow cooker makes for a much tastier stock. Drizzle the chicken and onion with a bit of olive oil and roast at 350°F for 30 to 40 minutes, or until light brown.

BEEF STOCK

MAKES 8 CUPS

PREP
20 MINUTES

COOK
30 MINUTES
IN THE OVEN
plus
8 HOURS
ON LOW

GLUTEN-FREE

SOY-FREE

NUT-FREE

For a richer, more deeply flavored beef stock, you must roast the bones and some of the vegetables before simmering all the ingredients in the slow cooker. You can skip this step if you'd like, but you'll lose the toasted richness roasting gives the final stock. Ask your butcher for meaty bones; he or she may just have some to give to you. If not, purchase knucklebones or meaty ribs. Homemade beef stock makes the most wonderful gravies, chilis, stews, and casseroles.

2 pounds meaty beef bones

1 onion, unpeeled and sliced

Extra-virgin olive oil, for drizzling

6 cups cool water, divided

2 garlic cloves, unpeeled and sliced

2 carrots, cut into chunks

1 celery stalk, sliced

1 tomato, chopped

1 teaspoon salt

4 peppercorns

1 bay leaf

½ teaspoon dried oregano leaves

1. Preheat the oven to 375°F.

2. Place the beef bones and the onion on a baking sheet with sides, and drizzle with olive oil. Roast for 20 to 30 minutes, or until the meat is browned.

3. Place the bones and onion in the slow cooker. Add ½ cup of water to the baking sheet and scrape to remove the pan drippings (that's where the flavor is). Then add the water with the scraped-up drippings to the slow cooker along with the remaining 5½ cups of water and the rest of the ingredients.

continued

4. Cover and cook on low for 7 to 8 hours, or until the stock looks rich and brown.

5. Strain the stock, pressing on the solids to remove all the liquid.

6. Refrigerate the stock overnight, and then remove and discard the layer of fat that accumulated on top.

7. Use immediately, refrigerate the stock for up to 4 days, or freeze in 1-cup portions for up to 4 months.

PER SERVING (1 cup) Calories: 31; Total fat: 0g; Saturated fat: 0g; Cholesterol: 0mg; Carbohydrates: 3g; Fiber: 0g; Protein: 5g

BONE BROTH

PREP
15 MINUTES

COOK
10 HOURS
ON LOW

GLUTEN-FREE

SOY-FREE

NUT-FREE

MAKES 8 CUPS

Bone broth has been around for ages, but its spike in popularity in recent years can be pinned to the growth of the Paleo diet, whose adherents eat a largely meat-and-vegetable-based diet and avoid grains, legumes, and dairy. Bone broth is very high in protein, minerals, and gelatin. As the bones cook, calcium, magnesium, phosphorus, and other minerals leach into the water. Beyond using the broth as the base for soups and gravies, many people drink it straight, either warm or cold, both to prevent and cure illness. This is technically a stock since it includes bones, but the recipe is widely known as broth, so we use the term here.

1 pound meaty beef bones or spareribs

1 carrot, cut into chunks

½ cup sliced mushrooms

1 onion, sliced

1-inch knob fresh ginger

2 garlic cloves, smashed

1 tablespoon chopped fresh chives

1 tablespoon apple cider vinegar

6½ cups cool water

1. In the slow cooker, combine all the ingredients.

2. Cover and cook on low for 9 to 10 hours, or until the broth is golden brown, skimming any foam off the surface occasionally.

3. Strain the broth through a fine-mesh strainer. You can strain it a second time through cheesecloth, if you'd like.

continued

4. Cover and refrigerate overnight, and then remove and discard the layer of fat that accumulates on top.

5. Use immediately, refrigerate the broth for up to 5 days, or freeze in 1-cup portions for up to 3 months.

PER SERVING (1 cup) Calories: 80; Total fat: 5g; Saturated fat: 1g; Cholesterol: 0mg; Carbohydrates: 0g; Fiber: 0g; Protein: 5g

PREP IT RIGHT Bones from cows that have been grass-fed are best but are not necessary. Ask your butcher at the supermarket about your options. You can also use turkey or chicken bones for a lighter broth.

ITALIAN TOMATO SAUCE

PREP
15 MINUTES

COOK
6 HOURS
ON LOW

GLUTEN-FREE

SOY-FREE

NUT-FREE

MAKES 8 CUPS

Fresh tomatoes, garlic, and onion, coupled with low and slow cooking, elevate this ubiquitous Italian tomato sauce into something extraordinary. It's so easy to make, and it freezes beautifully. Try adding some crushed red pepper flakes after the sauce is done if you'd like a little spiciness.

1 onion, chopped

3 garlic cloves, minced

2 large tomatoes, peeled and chopped

¼ cup tomato paste

1 (14-ounce) can diced tomatoes, undrained

1 (8-ounce) can tomato sauce

1 bay leaf

1 teaspoon dried oregano leaves

1 teaspoon dried basil leaves

½ teaspoon salt

1 teaspoon brown sugar

2 cups Chicken Stock (page 28) or Vegetable Broth (page 27)

1. In the slow cooker, combine all the ingredients and stir.

2. Cover and cook on low for 6 hours.

3. Remove and discard the bay leaf.

4. Cool the stock, and then serve, cover and refrigerate for up to 3 days, or freeze in 1-cup portions for up to 3 months.

PER SERVING (1 cup) Calories: 49; Total fat: 4g; Saturated fat: 0g; Cholesterol: 6mg; Carbohydrates: 9g; Fiber: 2g; Protein: 3g

MOLE SAUCE

PREP
15 MINUTES

COOK
6 HOURS
ON LOW

GLUTEN-FREE

SOY-FREE

MAKES 8 CUPS

This rich Mexican sauce, made with different types of dried and fresh chile peppers and cocoa powder for that familiar deep, smoky flavor, is traditionally made by roasting and grinding the ingredients, which can take at least a full day. Thank goodness you can enjoy this smooth, creamy sauce with just a bit of prep.

4 dried ancho chiles, stemmed

4 dried chipotle chiles, stemmed

3 corn tortillas, thinly sliced

3 cups Chicken Stock (page 28), divided

2 tomatoes, chopped

1 onion, chopped

⅓ cup peanut butter

5 garlic cloves, minced

2 jalapeño peppers, minced

1 tablespoon chili powder

½ teaspoon ground cumin

2 tablespoons cocoa powder

1 teaspoon dried oregano leaves

1 teaspoon salt

⅛ teaspoon freshly ground black pepper

1. In a blender or food processor, process the ancho chiles, chipotle chiles, tortillas, and 1 cup of stock until smooth.

2. Put the mixture in the slow cooker. Add the remaining 2 cups of stock and the remaining ingredients and stir to combine.

3. Cover and cook on low for 6 hours, or until the sauce has blended. At this point you can purée the sauce by using an immersion blender or leave it as is.

4. Cool for 30 minutes, and then serve, cover and refrigerate for up to 4 days, or freeze in ½-cup portions for up to 3 months.

PER SERVING (½ cup) Calories: 80; Total fat: 7g; Saturated fat: 1g; Cholesterol: 5mg; Carbohydrates: 9g; Fiber: 2g; Protein: 4g

PERFECT PAIR Use this mole to top roasted or grilled chicken, or add it to enchiladas or tacos. It's also wonderful as a dip for homemade quesadillas.

PREP
20 MINUTES

COOK
6 HOURS
ON LOW

GLUTEN-FREE

SOY-FREE

NUT-FREE

MARINARA SAUCE

MAKES 8 CUPS

Typically, marinara sauce calls for fresh tomatoes, carrots, and fresh basil—the tomatoes' acidity, the carrots' sweetness, and the basil's sweet-savory aromatics combine to make a simple yet exquisite sauce. Since fresh basil is a delicate herb, this recipe gives it a hearty boost by adding dried basil, which has a deeper, spicier note than fresh. This sauce is delicious served over hot cooked pasta or spread on pizza (not made in the slow cooker!).

5 large beefsteak tomatoes, peeled, seeded, and chopped

1 carrot, peeled and sliced

1 onion, chopped

4 garlic cloves, minced

1 bay leaf

1 teaspoon dried basil leaves

1 teaspoon brown sugar

1 teaspoon salt

⅛ teaspoon freshly ground black pepper

2½ cups Chicken Stock (page 28) or Vegetable Broth (page 27)

½ cup dry red wine (optional)

2 tablespoons minced fresh basil leaves

1. In the slow cooker, combine all the ingredients except the fresh basil leaves.

2. Cover and cook on low for 6 hours.

3. Remove and discard the bay leaf, and stir in the fresh basil.

4. Cool the sauce for 30 minutes, and then serve, cover and refrigerate for up to 4 days, or freeze in 1-cup portions for up to 4 months.

PER SERVING (1 cup) Calories: 57; Total fat: 5g; Saturated fat: 0g; Cholesterol: 8mg; Carbohydrates: 8g; Fiber: 2g; Protein: 3g

SEASONAL SUBSTITUTION This marinara is simply divine using heirloom tomatoes from the summertime farmers' market. There are many wonderful varieties to choose from, including Brandywine, Mortgage Lifter, Mr. Stripey, and German Johnson.

BOLOGNESE SAUCE

MAKES 8 CUPS

PREP
10 MINUTES

COOK
10 MINUTES
ON THE
STOVE TOP
plus
8 HOURS
ON LOW

GLUTEN-FREE

SOY-FREE

NUT-FREE

One of the classic Italian sauces, Bolognese has a rich mouthfeel that comes from the cream. This versatile recipe can be used with a variety of meats—try it with combinations of beef, pork, lamb, and bacon—and still deliver a complex, flavorful sauce. Bolognese does start on the stove top, since the beef must be browned first, but don't let that deter you; it will become a regular in your arsenal of go-to sauces. Use it in lasagna, or top linguine or fettuccine with it.

½ pound lean ground beef

½ pound pork sausage

1 onion, chopped

4 garlic cloves, minced

1 (14-ounce) can diced tomatoes, undrained

1 (8-ounce) can tomato sauce

1 cup Beef Stock (page 29)

2 tablespoons tomato paste

1 bay leaf

1 teaspoon dried oregano leaves

½ teaspoon dried basil leaves

½ teaspoon salt

⅛ teaspoon freshly ground black pepper

½ cup light cream

1. In a large skillet over medium heat, cook the ground beef, sausage, onion, and garlic, stirring to break up the meat until it browns, 8 to 10 minutes. Drain well.

2. In the slow cooker, combine the beef mixture with all the remaining ingredients except the cream.

3. Cover and cook on low for 8 hours.

4. After cooking is over, stir in the cream.

5. Cool the mixture for 30 minutes. Then remove and discard the bay leaf and serve immediately, cover and refrigerate for up to 3 days, or freeze in 1-cup portions for up to 4 months.

PER SERVING (1 cup) Calories: 200; Total fat: 12g; Saturated fat: 5g; Cholesterol: 57mg; Carbohydrates: 7g; Fiber: 2g; Protein: 16g

PREP
20 MINUTES

COOK
4 HOURS
ON LOW

GLUTEN-FREE

NUT-FREE

VEGAN

PINEAPPLE SALSA

MAKES 6 CUPS

Pineapple makes a delicious salsa: The sugars caramelize as they cook, giving it a sweetness that's hard to resist when coupled with savory onion and garlic and the heat of jalapeño. Try topping chicken, ham, or tacos with it.

1 (20-ounce) can unsweetened crushed pineapple, undrained

1 (20-ounce) can pineapple tidbits in juice, drained

2 onions, chopped

3 garlic cloves, minced

1 jalapeño pepper, minced

½ cup brown sugar

2 tablespoons honey

1 tablespoon soy sauce

2 tablespoons apple cider vinegar

1 teaspoon dried thyme leaves

¼ teaspoon salt

1. In the slow cooker, combine all the ingredients and stir well.

2. Cover and cook on low for 3 to 4 hours, or until the salsa is well blended.

3. Cool for 30 minutes, and then serve, cover and refrigerate for up to 4 days, or freeze in ½-cup portions for up to 3 months.

PER SERVING (½ cup) Calories: 41; Total fat: 0g; Saturated fat: 0g; Cholesterol: 0g Carbohydrates: 11g; Fiber: 1g; Protein: 0g

SALSA VERDE

MAKES 7 CUPS

Salsa verde, or green salsa, is a classic Mexican condiment made using tomatillos, a fruit covered with a papery green husk. Salsa verde has an irresistibly tart, lemony flavor that sings however you use it, from just dipping your tortilla chips into a bowl of refreshing green deliciousness to giving your burrito a satisfying tang or brightening up a plate of huevos rancheros. You can find tomatillos in most grocery stores.

2½ pounds tomatillos, husks removed, rinsed, and chopped

1 green bell pepper, chopped

2 onions, chopped

3 garlic cloves, minced

2 jalapeño peppers, minced

½ cup chopped fresh cilantro leaves

1 teaspoon salt

⅛ teaspoon freshly ground black pepper

1 cup Vegetable Broth (page 27) or water

1. In the slow cooker, combine all the ingredients and stir.

2. Cover and cook on low for 4 hours.

3. Cool and serve, refrigerate for up to 4 days, or freeze in ½-cup portions for up to 3 months.

PER SERVING (½ cup) Calories: 38; Total fat: 1g; Saturated fat: 0g; Cholesterol: 0g Carbohydrates: 7g; Fiber: 2g; Protein: 1g

NEXT DAY Use this flavorful, spicy cooked salsa to make Beef Fajitas (page 96), Chicken Tortilla Soup (page 65), or Steak and Black Bean Chili (page 70). Or use it as a condiment when you serve tacos. It's also delicious added to quesadillas or in pulled-pork sandwiches.

GLUTEN-FREE

SOY-FREE

NUT-FREE

VEGAN

BBQ SAUCE

MAKES 7 CUPS

If you're not one of those people who have a family barbecue sauce recipe that's been handed down over the generations, this recipe is the roadmap you need to create your own tradition. Add herbs or spices to make it as mild or spicy as you like, try different ketchup brands different types of chile, and even tinker with the sugar-to-honey ratio to make it your own. This sauce is delicious on steak, grilled chicken, and burgers. For a super-simple slow cooker meal, pour some over boneless, skinless chicken thighs.

3 cups ketchup

1 (8-ounce) can tomato sauce

½ cup Dijon mustard

3 tablespoons coarse ground mustard

1 onion, chopped

3 garlic cloves, minced

2 jalapeño peppers, minced

½ cup brown sugar

¼ cup honey

2 celery stalks, finely chopped

3 tablespoons chopped celery leaves

3 tablespoons freshly squeezed lemon juice

2 teaspoons chili powder

1 teaspoon ground smoked paprika

1 teaspoon salt

⅛ teaspoon freshly ground pepper

1. In the slow cooker, combine all the ingredients.

2. Cover and cook on low for 6 to 7 hours.

3. Cool and serve, cover and refrigerate for up to 4 days, or freeze in 1-cup portions for up to 4 months.

PER SERVING (1 cup) Calories: 216; Total fat: 2g; Saturated fat: 0g; Cholesterol: 0mg; Carbohydrates: 52g; Fiber: 2g; Protein: 4g

 DID YOU KNOW? When buying ketchup for this recipe, look for brands without high-fructose corn syrup (HFCS). HFCS is an inexpensive and highly processed substitute for real sugar.

RED SALSA

PREP
20 MINUTES

COOK
5 HOURS
ON LOW

GLUTEN-FREE

SOY-FREE

NUT-FREE

VEGAN

MAKES 7 CUPS

Tangy tomatoes and spicy chiles marry to make a delicious salsa that's great on enchiladas and tacos as well as in chilis and soups. Serve a big bowl of this salsa with some chips for a simple game-day crowd pleaser.

2 onions, chopped

8 large tomatoes, chopped

3 celery stalks, sliced

5 garlic cloves, minced

2 dried ancho chiles, broken into pieces

2 jalapeño chiles, minced

½ cup water

2 teaspoons chili powder

1 teaspoon salt

⅛ teaspoon freshly ground black pepper

1. In the slow cooker, combine all the ingredients.

2. Cover and cook on low for 5 hours.

3. Either purée using an immersion blender or leave the salsa chunky.

4. Cool and serve, cover and refrigerate for up to 4 days, or freeze in ½-cup portions for up to 3 months.

PER SERVING (½ cup) Calories: 36; Total fat: 0g; Saturated fat: 0g; Cholesterol: 0mg; Carbohydrates: 8g; Fiber: 2g; Protein: 2g

PREP
20 MINUTES

COOK
6 HOURS
ON LOW

GLUTEN-FREE

SOY-FREE

NUT-FREE

VEGAN

CHUTNEY

MAKES 7 CUPS

Chutney can be purchased at many stores, but it's so easy to make—and tastes so much better homemade—that there's no reason not to create your own. Substitute whatever fruits you like in this versatile, tasty recipe.

3 onions, chopped

5 garlic cloves, sliced

1 (20-ounce) can pineapple tidbits, drained

2 mangoes, peeled and chopped

2 Granny Smith apples, peeled and chopped

1 cup golden raisins

1 red bell pepper, minced

½ cup brown sugar

2 tablespoons freshly squeezed lemon juice

1 tablespoon minced fresh ginger

2 teaspoons Curry Rub (page 23)

1 teaspoon salt

½ teaspoon ground cinnamon

⅛ teaspoon ground allspice

½ cup chopped fresh cilantro

1. In the slow cooker, combine all the ingredients except the cilantro.

2. Cover and cook on low for 5 to 6 hours, or until blended and all the fruit is soft. Stir in the cilantro.

3. Cool and serve, cover and refrigerate for up to 4 days, or freeze in 1/2-cup portions for up to 4 months.

PER SERVING (½ cup) Calories: 121; Total fat: 0g; Saturated fat: 0g; Cholesterol: 0mg; Carbohydrates: 31g; Fiber: 3g; Protein: 1g

 PREP IT RIGHT Preparing a mango can be tricky. Make sure the mango gives slightly when you press on it, indicating that it's ripe. Stand the mango on end, and slice down both wide sides, avoiding the pit. Score the flesh into squares, and then, using your thumbs, push up against the skin to "pop" the scored flesh outward so that the squares fan out. Use your fingers or a knife to remove the flesh.

PREP
20 MINUTES

COOK
8 HOURS
ON LOW

GLUTEN-FREE

SOY-FREE

NUT-FREE

TOMATO RELISH

MAKES 7 CUPS

Some might say that tomato relish is a little old-school, but there's nothing old-fashioned about sweet and spicy flavors that make for an irresistible palate pleaser. And it is so versatile: Use the relish to accompany grilled meats and poultry, as a spread on sandwiches, or even added to meatloaf. For the best results, use only in-season tomatoes to make this recipe.

5 large tomatoes, seeded and chopped

2 onions, chopped

2 red bell peppers, chopped

3 garlic cloves, minced

1 cup apple cider vinegar

1 cup brown sugar

1 cup granulated sugar

½ cup honey

¼ cup Dijon mustard

2 teaspoons celery seed

2 teaspoons salt

½ teaspoon freshly ground pepper

1. In the slow cooker, combine all the ingredients and stir.

2. Cover and cook on low for 8 hours, stirring once during cooking time.

3. Cool and serve, cover and refrigerate for up to 4 days, or freeze in ½-cup portions for up to 3 months.

PER SERVING (½ cup) Calories: 162; Total fat: 1g; Saturated fat: 0g; Cholesterol: 0mg; Carbohydrates: 40g; Fiber: 2g; Protein: 1g

PERFECT PAIR The relish is delicious on roast beef sandwiches or as a condiment with poached chicken or grilled steak. Try it also on tacos or enchiladas for a sweeter taste, or use it in place of ketchup on a burger.

CRANBERRY SAUCE

MAKES 7 CUPS

Cranberry sauce is one of the classic condiments at any Thanksgiving table, but it's delicious served over grilled chicken or pork anytime. Tangy, fresh cranberries coupled with crisp Granny Smith apples are tamed with delicate pears, refreshing citrus, and a touch of cinnamon and sugar to give you a sweet sauce you'll reach for often.

2 (12-ounce) packages fresh cranberries

2 Granny Smith apples, peeled and chopped

2 pears, peeled and chopped

1 cup brown sugar

1/3 cup orange juice

2 tablespoons freshly squeezed lemon juice

2 teaspoons orange zest

2 teaspoons ground cinnamon

1/2 teaspoon salt

1. In the slow cooker, combine all the ingredients and stir.

2. Cover and cook on low for 8 hours, or until the cranberries have popped and the sauce is slightly thickened.

3. Cool and serve, cover and refrigerate for up to 4 days, or freeze in 1/2-cup portions for up to 4 months.

PER SERVING (½ cup) Calories: 101; Total fat: 0g; Saturated fat: 0g; Cholesterol: 0mg; Carbohydrates: 24g; Fiber: 4g; Protein: 0g

THREE

SOUPS, STEWS & CHILIS

From a classic lentil vegetable soup to a chickpea tagine and bouillabaisse, the slow cooker is great for one-pot soups, stews, and chilis from all over the globe. All you need to complete your meal is a green or fruit salad and some bread or dinner rolls. What could be easier?

POTATO SOUP WITH SPINACH

PREP
20 MINUTES

COOK
8 HOURS
ON LOW

GLUTEN-FREE

SOY-FREE

NUT-FREE

VEGETARIAN

SERVES 2

Just because potato soup is one of the most inexpensive soups you can make doesn't mean it tastes cheap. This recipe tastes rich and hearty. The silky soup, complemented by the wilted spinach, melts in your mouth. Add a hunk of country bread, and you just made your meal extra hearty and heavenly.

4 cups Vegetable Broth (page 27)

2 russet potatoes, peeled and cubed

1 onion, chopped

½ cup chopped leeks

2 garlic cloves, minced

½ teaspoon salt

½ teaspoon dried marjoram

⅛ teaspoon freshly ground black pepper

2 cups baby spinach leaves

1. In the slow cooker, combine the broth, potatoes, onion, leeks, garlic, salt, marjoram, and pepper, and stir.

2. Cover and cook on low for 7½ hours.

3. Using an immersion blender or potato masher, blend or mash the ingredients so the soup is fairly smooth but still has texture.

4. Add the spinach, cover, and cook on low for another 20 to 30 minutes, or until the spinach is wilted.

5. Ladle the soup into 2 bowls and serve.

PER SERVING Calories: 225; Total fat: 1g; Saturated fat: 0g; Cholesterol: 0mg; Carbohydrates: 53g; Fiber: 8g; Protein: 6g

GLUTEN-FREE

SOY-FREE

NUT-FREE

VEGAN

LENTIL-VEGETABLE SOUP

SERVES 2

Lentils have a fabulous nutty flavor and become tender and soft during cooking. Add tangy grape tomatoes and sweet carrots, and you have a healthy, deeply satisfying winner.

½ cup dried lentils

1 cup chopped grape tomatoes

2 carrots, chopped

2 celery stalks, chopped

1 onion, chopped

3 garlic cloves, sliced

1 bay leaf

½ teaspoon dried thyme leaves

½ teaspoon dried marjoram

½ teaspoon salt

2 cups Vegetable Broth (page 27)

1 cup water

2 tablespoons minced fresh thyme leaves

1. Sort the lentils and rinse; drain well.

2. In the slow cooker, combine the lentils with all the remaining ingredients except the fresh thyme leaves.

3. Cover and cook on low for 8 hours, or until the lentils and vegetables are tender.

4. Remove and discard the bay leaf, stir in the fresh thyme leaves, ladle the soup into 2 bowls and serve.

PER SERVING Calories: 291; Total fat: 2g; Saturated fat: 1g; Cholesterol: 0mg; Carbohydrates: 49g; Fiber: 20g; Protein: 20g

DID YOU KNOW? There are many different types of lentils. Choose which one works best for your dish depending on the characteristics you want in it. Brown lentils will become soft during long cooking time and so are ideal for soup. French Puy, or green lentils, have a slightly spicy taste and stay firm during cooking. Red lentils have a sweet flavor and become very soft during long cooking times.

TOMATO SOUP

SERVES 2

PREP
15 MINUTES

COOK
7 HOURS
ON LOW

GLUTEN-FREE

SOY-FREE

NUT-FREE

VEGAN

Tomato soup is all about, well, the tomatoes, so use the best quality you can find. San Marzano tomatoes from Italy should be your first choice. Fire-roasted canned tomatoes are also a good option. The soup is delicious as a first course, or it could be the main course for lunch, served with muffins or garlic bread and a fruit salad. Tomato soup is delicious year round.

1 (28-ounce) can whole tomatoes, undrained

1 onion, chopped

½ cup shredded carrot

½ cup chopped celery stalk

3 garlic cloves, minced

2 cups Vegetable Broth (page 27)

1 teaspoon dried basil leaves

½ teaspoon salt

⅛ teaspoon freshly ground black pepper

1 tablespoon minced fresh thyme leaves

1. In the slow cooker, combine all the ingredients except the fresh thyme leaves.

2. Cover and cook on low for 7 hours.

3. Purée the soup using an immersion blender, or purée in small batches in a food processor or blender.

4. Ladle the soup into 2 bowls, garnish with the fresh thyme leaves, and serve.

PER SERVING Calories: 158; Total fat: 2g; Saturated fat: 1g; Cholesterol: 0mg; Carbohydrates: 27g; Fiber: 8g; Protein: 10g

SEASONAL SUBSTITUTION This soup is even better with garden-fresh or farmers' market tomatoes. Peel and seed the tomatoes before adding to the slow cooker. To peel, cut an "X" in the blossom end of each tomato, and drop into boiling water for 10 seconds. Using tongs, remove the tomatoes and plunge into ice water, and then peel off the skin.

SPLIT PEA SOUP WITH HAM

SERVES 2

PREP
15 MINUTES

COOK
7 HOURS
ON LOW

GLUTEN-FREE

SOY-FREE

NUT-FREE

Split peas—peas literally split in half—come in green and yellow, and you can find them in any grocery store. They cook up into a gorgeous potage with the most tender, silky texture. A bright dash of lemon juice and sweet-salty ham make this a delicious soup that will warm you up on any cold winter day.

1½ cups dried split peas

1 onion, chopped

2 garlic cloves, minced

1 bay leaf

1 cup chopped cooked ham

4 cups Chicken Stock (page 28)

½ teaspoon dried thyme leaves

1 tablespoon freshly squeezed lemon juice

⅛ teaspoon freshly ground black pepper

1 cup garlic croutons

1. Sort the peas to remove any twigs, dirt, or stones. Rinse well and drain.

2. In the slow cooker, combine the peas, onion, garlic, bay leaf, ham, stock, thyme, lemon juice, and pepper, and stir.

3. Cover and cook on low for 7 hours, or until the split peas dissolve and the soup is thick.

4. Remove the bay leaf, ladle the soup into 2 bowls, top with the croutons, and serve.

PER SERVING Calories: 571; Total fat: 37g; Saturated fat: 3g; Cholesterol: 89mg; Carbohydrates: 95g; Fiber: 36g; Protein: 56g

SEASONAL SUBSTITUTION If you have a ham bone left over from a special dinner, like Easter or Christmas, use it in this recipe in place of the chopped cooked ham. The bone will add a wonderful depth of flavor to the soup. When the soup is done, take the bone out and remove any meat. Chop the meat and return it to the soup.

TUSCAN BEAN SOUP WITH HERBS

SERVES 2

Thyme, rosemary, and parsley give mild navy beans an aromatic kick in this soup. The beans soften perfectly, becoming tender and sweet.

1 cup dried navy beans

1 onion, chopped

2 garlic cloves, minced

2 carrots, sliced

2 Yukon Gold potatoes, cubed

3 cups Vegetable Broth (page 27)

½ teaspoon salt

⅛ teaspoon freshly ground black pepper

½ teaspoon dried thyme leaves

2 cups baby spinach leaves

2 teaspoons chopped fresh rosemary leaves

2 tablespoons chopped fresh flat-leaf parsley

2 tablespoons extra-virgin olive oil, divided

1. Sort the beans and rinse; drain well.

2. In the slow cooker, combine the beans, onion, garlic, carrots, potatoes, broth, salt, pepper, and thyme.

3. Cover and cook on low for 7½ hours.

4. Add the spinach, rosemary, and parsley to the slow cooker and stir. Cover and cook on low for 25 to 30 minutes more, or until the spinach wilts.

5. Ladle the soup into 2 bowls, drizzle each with 1 tablespoon of olive oil, and serve.

PER SERVING Calories: 551; Total fat: 17g; Saturated fat: 3g; Cholesterol: 0mg; Carbohydrates: 88g; Fiber: 25g; Protein: 29g

DID YOU KNOW? If you're prone to digestive discomfort after eating beans, soaking dried beans before cooking can ease any issues. Sort the beans, rinse them, then place in a large bowl and cover with cool water. Let stand overnight. In the morning, drain and rinse the beans as directed in the recipe, discarding the soaking water. Preparing the beans in this manner helps rid them of some of their indigestible sugars.

PREP
20 MINUTES

COOK
8 HOURS
ON LOW

GLUTEN-FREE

SOY-FREE

NUT-FREE

GREEN CHICKEN CHILI

SERVES 2

This chili's light green color may look cooling, but watch out for those jalapeños! They add a delicious heat that pairs well with the mellow, citrusy taste of the tomatillos. If you like your chili really hot, add more jalapeño peppers, or try a Scotch bonnet for true heat.

5 boneless, skinless chicken thighs

½ teaspoon ground cumin

1 onion, chopped

4 tomatillos, husks removed, rinsed, and chopped

2 jalapeño peppers, minced

1 cup Salsa Verde (page 39)

1 (15-ounce) can cannellini beans, rinsed and drained

2 cups Chicken Stock (page 28)

½ teaspoon salt

⅛ teaspoon ground cayenne pepper

1. Sprinkle the chicken thighs with the cumin.

2. In the slow cooker, combine the chicken with the remaining ingredients and stir.

3. Cover and cook on low for 8 hours, or until the chicken is tender.

4. Remove the chicken from the slow cooker and shred; return to the slow cooker and stir.

5. Ladle the chili into 2 bowls and serve.

PER SERVING Calories: 535; Total fat: 24g; Saturated fat: 1g; Cholesterol: 200mg; Carbohydrates: 46g; Fiber: 10g; Protein: 60g

PERFECT PAIR Serve this spicy chili with tortilla chips, cool sour cream, and chopped fresh cilantro. The contrast between the hot chili, cool sour cream, crisp chips, and bright cilantro is wonderful.

PREP
20 MINUTES

COOK
8 HOURS
ON LOW

SOY-FREE

NUT-FREE

VEGETARIAN

PASTA E FAGIOLI

SERVES 2

With tangy tomatoes, tender beans and carrots, and aromatic herbs, this classic Italian soup is the ultimate comfort food. Serve it with garlic bread and a green salad, and you'll think a real Italian *nonna* (grandmother) was in the kitchen taking care of you.

1 onion, chopped

2 carrots, sliced

2 celery stalks, sliced

3 garlic cloves, minced

1 (15-ounce) can red kidney beans, rinsed and drained

1 (14-ounce) can diced tomatoes, undrained

2 cups Vegetable Broth (page 27)

½ teaspoon dried oregano

½ teaspoon dried basil

½ teaspoon dried thyme

½ teaspoon salt

½ cup small shell pasta

¼ cup grated Parmesan cheese, divided

1. In the slow cooker, combine the onion, carrots, celery, garlic, beans, tomatoes, broth, oregano, basil, thyme, and salt.

2. Cover and cook on low for 7½ hours, or until the vegetables are tender.

3. Add the pasta and stir well. Cover and cook on low for 30 minutes more, or until the pasta is tender.

4. Ladle the soup into 2 bowls, top each with ⅛ cup of grated Parmesan, and serve.

PER SERVING Calories: 456; Total fat: 6g; Saturated fat: 3g; Cholesterol: 10mg; Carbohydrates: 74g; Fiber: 16g; Protein: 29g

SEASONAL SUBSTITUTION This recipe is perfect on cool summer nights; just substitute fresh chopped tomatoes for the canned tomatoes, and use summer squash and zucchini in place of the carrots and celery.

CHICKEN AVGOLEMONO

SERVES 2

PREP
15 MINUTES

COOK
7 HOURS
ON LOW
plus
15 MINUTES
ON HIGH

GLUTEN-FREE

SOY-FREE

NUT-FREE

The crisp acidity of lemon juice and the lusciousness of both sour and heavy creams turn this refurbished Greek stunner into something you'll want to make week after week. Served with warm, crisp bread, it makes for a satisfying meal.

2 bone-in, skinless chicken breasts

3⅔ cups Chicken Stock (page 28)

1 onion, chopped

2 garlic cloves, minced

1 carrot, chopped

⅓ cup basmati rice

½ teaspoon salt

½ cup heavy cream

¼ cup sour cream

3 tablespoons freshly squeezed lemon juice

1 tablespoon cornstarch

1. In the slow cooker, combine the chicken, stock, onion, garlic, carrot, rice, and salt. Stir well.

2. Cover and cook on low for 6½ hours.

3. Remove the chicken from the soup. Remove the meat from the bones, and discard the bones or save them for stock. Shred the chicken and return it to the soup.

4. In a medium bowl, whisk together the cream, sour cream, lemon juice, and cornstarch. Add 1 cup of hot liquid from the soup and whisk well.

5. Beat the cream mixture into the soup and cook on high for 15 minutes, or until the soup is slightly thickened.

6. Ladle the soup into 2 bowls and serve.

PER SERVING Calories: 665; Total fat: 50g; Saturated fat: 14g; Cholesterol: 195mg; Carbohydrates: 52g; Fiber: 3g; Protein: 52g

THAI CHICKEN–COCONUT SOUP

SERVES 2

Known as *tom kha gai* in its native Thailand, this soup combines spicy flavors from heady curry and tart ginger, sweet undertones from the coconut milk, and a fresh burst of liveliness from the lime zest and juice. You can find Thai fish sauce, or *nuoc nam*, in most large grocery stores.

5 boneless, skinless chicken thighs

1 cup sliced shiitake or cremini mushrooms

2 garlic cloves, minced

2 teaspoons grated fresh ginger

½ teaspoon lime zest

2 cups Chicken Stock (page 28)

1 cup coconut milk

1 tablespoon freshly squeezed lime juice

1 tablespoon Thai fish sauce

1 teaspoon curry powder

1 cup fresh snap peas

½ red bell pepper, cut with spiral cutter, if desired

¼ cucumber, cut with spiral cutter, if desired

1. In the slow cooker, combine all the ingredients except the snap peas, bell pepper, and cucumber.

2. Cover and cook on low for 7½ hours, or until the chicken is tender.

3. Remove the chicken from the soup and shred; return the chicken to the slow cooker.

4. Add the snap peas to the slow cooker, cover, and cook on low for 20 minutes more, until crisp-tender.

5. Ladle the soup into 2 bowls and serve. Garnish with the spiral-cut red bell pepper and cucumber.

PER SERVING Calories: 640; Total fat: 54g; Saturated fat: 29g; Cholesterol: 238mg; Carbohydrates: 17g; Fiber: 5g; Protein: 61g

PREP
15 MINUTES

COOK
7½ HOURS
ON LOW
plus
30 MINUTES
ON HIGH

GLUTEN-FREE

SOY-FREE

NUT-FREE

CHICKEN STEW WITH GNOCCHI

SERVES 2

Sometimes the simplest dishes taste the best; this soup is one of those. Succulent chicken, oniony leek, lush sweet potato, and tender gnocchi all come together in the perfect filling dinner. Make sure your leek is well rinsed before you add it, as leeks can be sandy. To clean, rinse, pull off the tough outer leaves, and halve lengthwise. Chop the leek, put it in a bowl of cool water, and agitate the water with your hand; the sand will fall to the bottom. Scoop the leek out of the bowl with a slotted spoon or a sieve, dump out the dirty water, and repeat with a fresh batch of cool water.

4 boneless, skinless chicken thighs, cubed

1 leek, white part only, chopped

2 garlic cloves, minced

1 sweet potato, peeled and chopped

½ cup chopped tomato

½ teaspoon salt

½ teaspoon dried basil leaves

⅛ teaspoon freshly ground black pepper

3 cups Chicken Stock (page 28)

1 cup potato gnocchi

1. In the slow cooker, combine all the ingredients except the gnocchi.

2. Cover and cook on low for 7½ hours.

3. Add the gnocchi. Cover and cook on high for 25 to 30 minutes more, or until the gnocchi are tender.

4. Ladle the stew into 2 bowls and serve.

PER SERVING Calories: 434; Total fat: 31g; Saturated fat: 3g; Cholesterol: 208mg; Carbohydrates: 35g; Fiber: 3g; Protein: 53g

DID YOU KNOW? Most grocery stores stock potato gnocchi in shelf-stable packages that don't need refrigeration. Look for it in the pasta aisle. After you open the package, you can freeze the remainder and add it to soups as needed.

CHICKEN AND SHRIMP BOUILLABAISSE

SERVES 2

PREP
20 MINUTES

COOK
7 HOURS
ON LOW
plus
20 MINUTES
ON HIGH

GLUTEN-FREE

SOY-FREE

NUT-FREE

Bouillabaisse, a French stew from Marseille, originates from a word that means "to boil" and "to reduce heat." The three kinds of fish typically used in this stew aren't available in the United States, but this version—using chicken and shrimp—is just as satisfying.

4 boneless, skinless chicken thighs, cut into strips

1 onion, chopped

3 garlic cloves, minced

1 cup sliced fennel

2 large tomatoes, seeded and chopped

2 Yukon Gold potatoes, cubed

2 cups clam juice

½ cup dry white wine

1 teaspoon dried thyme leaves

½ teaspoon salt

⅛ teaspoon freshly ground black pepper

1 pinch saffron

½ pound medium shrimp, peeled and deveined

1 teaspoon minced fresh rosemary leaves

1. In the slow cooker, combine all the ingredients except the shrimp and rosemary, and mix well.

2. Cover and cook on low for 7 hours.

3. Add the shrimp and rosemary. Cover and cook on high for 20 minutes, or until the shrimp curl and turn pink.

4. Ladle the stew into 2 bowls and serve.

PER SERVING Calories: 720; Total fat: 15g; Saturated fat: 0g; Cholesterol: 383mg; Carbohydrates: 76g; Fiber: 9g; Protein: 70g

PERFECT PAIR Bouillabaisse is usually served with rouille, a spicy garlic mayonnaise made with roasted red peppers. To make it, buy a jar of roasted red peppers. Purée 1 pepper, 2 garlic cloves, ½ cup mayonnaise, 1 teaspoon freshly squeezed lemon juice, and a pinch of crushed red pepper flakes in a blender or food processor until smooth. Refrigerate any leftovers.

PREP
15 MINUTES

COOK
8 HOURS
ON LOW

GLUTEN-FREE

SOY-FREE

NUT-FREE

WILD RICE–MEATBALL SOUP

SERVES 2

Wild rice has a wonderful nutty taste and slightly chewy texture that goes wonderfully with meatballs. And because it is a grass seed (and actually not a type of rice), it takes a while to cook, making it perfect for the slow cooker. Wild rice grows wild in marshes in northern Minnesota and Wisconsin.

½ pound frozen fully cooked meatballs

1 onion, chopped

2 large tomatoes, seeded and chopped

2 garlic cloves, minced

½ cup wild rice, rinsed

1 carrot, sliced

3 cups Beef Stock (page 29)

1 bay leaf

½ teaspoon dried marjoram leaves

½ teaspoon salt

⅛ teaspoon freshly ground black pepper

1. In the slow cooker, combine all the ingredients.

2. Cover and cook on low for 8 hours, or until the vegetables are tender.

3. Remove the bay leaf, ladle the soup into 2 bowls, and serve.

PER SERVING Calories: 546; Total fat: 22g; Saturated fat: 8g; Cholesterol: 60mg; Carbohydrates: 53g; Fiber: 8g; Protein: 33g

INDIAN CAULIFLOWER-POTATO SOUP

SERVES 2

PREP
20 MINUTES

COOK
8 HOURS
ON LOW

GLUTEN-FREE

SOY-FREE

NUT-FREE

VEGETARIAN

Known as *aloo gobi* in India, this soup is well worth the time, with chunky potatoes and cauliflower florets giving it a hearty texture and curry paste and ginger adding a punchy zing. You can find curry paste at most large grocery stores. In place of the usual curry leaves, we'll use a bay leaf here.

1 onion, chopped

2 garlic cloves, sliced

2 teaspoons grated fresh ginger

1 tablespoon green curry paste

2 Yukon Gold potatoes, peeled and cubed

2 cups cauliflower florets

3 cups Vegetable Broth (page 27)

1 bay leaf

½ teaspoon salt

⅛ teaspoon freshly ground black pepper

½ cup light cream

1. In the slow cooker, combine all the ingredients except the light cream.

2. Cover and cook on low for 8 hours.

3. Remove and discard the bay leaf.

4. Using an immersion blender or potato masher, blend or mash the soup until just a bit of texture remains.

5. Stir in the cream, ladle the soup into 2 bowls, and serve.

PER SERVING Calories: 316; Total fat: 12g; Saturated fat: 6g; Cholesterol: 33mg; Carbohydrates: 49g; Fiber: 8g; Protein: 8g

DID YOU KNOW? There are three kinds of curry paste: green, yellow, and red. Read the label to make sure you're buying a vegetarian version if that's important to you, because some use shrimp. In general, yellow curry paste is mildest, made with some dried spices such as turmeric. Red curry paste is medium heat, made with dried red chiles, lemongrass, and kaffir. Green curry paste is the hottest and includes fresh green chiles, shallots, and coriander.

CHICKEN TORTILLA SOUP

SERVES 2

PREP
15 MINUTES

COOK
7½ HOURS
ON LOW
plus
30 MINUTES
ON HIGH

GLUTEN-FREE

SOY-FREE

NUT-FREE

Soups thickened with corn tortillas, like this classic Mexican dish, have a lush richness that is hard to resist. You can make this soup as spicy or as mild as you like by adjusting the number of chipotle peppers and amount of cayenne pepper.

5 boneless, skinless chicken thighs, cubed

1 russet potato, peeled and cubed

1 onion, chopped

1 carrot, sliced

2 stalks celery, sliced

2 garlic cloves, minced

1 chipotle pepper in adobo sauce, minced

1 cup frozen corn

2 cups Chicken Stock (page 28)

2 teaspoons chili powder

½ teaspoon salt

¼ teaspoon ground cumin

⅛ teaspoon ground cayenne pepper

2 (6-inch) corn tortillas, cut into strips, divided

1. In the slow cooker, combine all the ingredients except the tortillas.

2. Cover and cook for 7½ hours on low.

3. Add half of the tortilla strips and stir. Cover and cook on high for another 30 minutes, or until the tortillas have almost dissolved.

4. Stir again, ladle into 2 bowls, and serve topped with the remaining tortilla strips.

PER SERVING Calories: 616; Total fat: 25g; Saturated fat: 3g; Cholesterol: 195mg; Carbohydrates: 69g; Fiber: 18g; Protein: 64g

PERFECT PAIR Serve this rich, spicy soup with cold sour cream, cubed avocado or homemade guacamole, chopped cilantro, and chopped cherry tomatoes.

FRENCH VEGETABLE STEW

SERVES 2

Originally from Nice, France, this stew is chock-full of good-for-you veggies like peppers, squash, eggplant, and tomatoes. Serve it with lots of crusty French bread for dipping.

1 small eggplant, peeled and cubed

1 onion, chopped

2 large tomatoes, seeded and chopped

1 red bell pepper, chopped

1 yellow bell pepper, chopped

1 small yellow summer squash, chopped

2 garlic cloves, minced

½ teaspoon dried basil leaves

½ teaspoon dried thyme leaves

½ teaspoon salt

⅛ teaspoon freshly ground black pepper

¼ cup dry white wine

2 cups Vegetable Broth (page 27)

2 tablespoons extra-virgin olive oil, divided

1. In the slow cooker, combine all the ingredients except the olive oil, and stir well.

2. Cover and cook on low for 7 hours.

3. Ladle the stew into 2 bowls, drizzle each with 1 tablespoon of olive oil, and serve.

PER SERVING Calories: 346; Total fat: 17g; Saturated fat: 3g; Cholesterol: 0mg; Carbohydrates: 38g; Fiber: 15g; Protein: 11g

VIETNAMESE BEEF AND NOODLE SOUP

SERVES 2

PREP
15 MINUTES

COOK
7½ HOURS
ON LOW
plus
20 MINUTES
ON HIGH

SOY-FREE

NUT-FREE

Known as pho (and pronounced *fuh*), this soup has elements of both hot and sour from ginger, fish sauce, hot chiles, and herbs. It's great served with a cold bottle of beer and some fruit salad for a cooling contrast.

½ pound chuck eye roast, cut into 1-inch pieces

1 onion, chopped

3 radishes, sliced

3 garlic cloves, minced

1 serrano chile, minced

1 tablespoon grated fresh ginger

1 tablespoon freshly squeezed lime juice

2 teaspoons fish sauce

1 star anise pod

3 cups Beef Stock (page 29)

½ teaspoon dried basil leaves

½ teaspoon dried marjoram leaves

½ teaspoon salt

¼ teaspoon freshly ground black pepper

½ (12-ounce) package udon noodles or spaghetti

1 tablespoon minced fresh basil leaves

1 tablespoon minced fresh mint

1. In the slow cooker, combine the beef, onion, radishes, garlic, chile, ginger, lime juice, fish sauce, star anise, stock, basil, marjoram, salt, and pepper.

2. Cover and cook on low for 7½ hours.

3. Add the udon noodles and stir. Cover and cook on high for 20 minutes, or until the noodles are tender.

4. Stir in the fresh basil and mint, ladle the soup into 2 bowls, and serve.

PER SERVING Calories: 432; Total fat: 5g; Saturated fat: 1g; Cholesterol: 22mg; Carbohydrates: 73g; Fiber: 7g; Protein: 29g

PREP
20 MINUTES

COOK
7 HOURS
ON LOW

GLUTEN-FREE

SOY-FREE

NUT-FREE

CHICKPEA TAGINE

SERVES 2

In addition to being a delicious North African stew, a tagine is also the cooking vessel—a shallow, round base and a conical top—in which that dish is made. The tagine is filled with the ingredients and then set over coals. This variation, made in the slow cooker, is less complicated—but just as delicious.

1 onion, chopped

2 garlic cloves, minced

1 (15-ounce) can chickpeas, rinsed and drained

1 large sweet potato, peeled and cubed

1 zucchini, peeled, seeded, and chopped

1 large tomato, seeded and chopped

2 cups Chicken Stock (page 28)

1 tablespoon freshly squeezed lemon juice

½ teaspoon salt

½ teaspoon lemon zest

¼ teaspoon ground cinnamon

⅛ teaspoon freshly ground black pepper

Pinch saffron threads

1. In the slow cooker, combine all the ingredients and stir.

2. Cover and cook on low for 7 hours, or until the squash and potatoes are tender.

3. Ladle the stew into 2 bowls and serve.

PER SERVING Calories: 331; Total fat: 3g; Saturated fat: 0g; Cholesterol: 0mg; Carbohydrates: 62g; Fiber: 13g; Protein: 15g

PREP IT RIGHT To seed a tomato, cut it in half through its "equator," halfway between the stem end and the blossom end. Gently squeeze the halves, removing the seeds and the tomato "jelly." Discard the seeds and jelly, and then chop the flesh.

SPICY BEEF CHILI

PREP
15 MINUTES

COOK
10 MINUTES
ON THE
STOVE TOP
plus
9 HOURS
ON LOW

GLUTEN-FREE

SOY-FREE

NUT-FREE

SERVES 2

Traditionally, true chili is made with just vegetables, tomatoes, and lots of cubed beef, but no beans. This recipe honors beef by really making it the centerpiece of the the chili, while kicking the heat up a notch with minced jalapeño. Enjoy any leftovers the next day by adding a bit of shredded cheese to them and making stove-top quesadillas in a skillet.

½ pound lean ground beef

1 onion, chopped

2 celery stalks, sliced

2 garlic cloves, minced

1 jalapeño chile, minced

1 (14-ounce) can diced tomatoes, undrained

1 cup Bone Broth (page 31) or Beef Stock (page 29)

2 teaspoons chili powder

½ teaspoon ground cumin

½ teaspoon salt

⅛ teaspoon freshly ground black pepper

1. In a medium saucepan over medium heat, cook the ground beef with the onion, stirring to break up the meat, until the beef is browned, about 10 minutes. Drain well.

2. In the slow cooker, combine the beef and onions with all the remaining ingredients and stir well.

3. Cover and cook on low for 9 hours, or until the chili is blended.

4. Ladle the chili into 2 bowls and serve.

PER SERVING Calories: 475; Total fat: 9g; Saturated fat: 3g; Cholesterol: 101mg; Carbohydrates: 50g; Fiber: 17g; Protein: 50g

PREP
15 MINUTES

COOK
7 HOURS
ON LOW
plus
30 MINUTES
ON HIGH

GLUTEN-FREE

SOY-FREE

NUT-FREE

STEAK AND BLACK BEAN CHILI

SERVES 2

While a traditional chili doesn't have beans, no one says you have to be traditional when you make chili in the home. This is a thick and hearty dish at its finest. The beans add nutrition and a chewy bite when paired with the cooked down steak and soft tomatoes. To cut the spiciness, serve with cool sour cream, crunchy chopped fresh onion, and smooth chopped avocado.

1 pound sirloin tip steak, cubed

1 onion, chopped

2 garlic cloves, minced

1 jalapeño pepper, minced

1 chipotle chili in adobo sauce, minced

2 tablespoons adobo sauce

1 (15-ounce) can black beans, rinsed and drained

1 (15-ounce) can diced tomatoes with green chiles

1 (8-ounce) can tomato sauce

1 teaspoons chili powder

½ teaspoon dried oregano

½ teaspoon salt

⅛ teaspoon freshly ground black pepper

⅛ teaspoon ground cayenne pepper

1 tablespoon cornstarch

¼ cup water

1. In the slow cooker, combine all the ingredients except the cornstarch and water, and stir.

2. Cover and cook on low for 7 hours.

3. In a small bowl, stir together the cornstarch and water. Stir the mixture into the slow cooker.

4. Cover and cook on high for 20 to 30 minutes, or until thickened, and serve.

PER SERVING Calories: 766; Total fat: 21g; Saturated fat: 7g; Cholesterol: 161mg; Carbohydrates: 67g; Fiber: 20g; Protein: 79g

MOROCCAN LAMB STEW

PREP
20 MINUTES

COOK
8 HOURS
ON LOW

GLUTEN-FREE

SOY-FREE

NUT-FREE

SERVES 2

Coriander, cinnamon, fennel, cumin, and pepper infuse this rich, thick stew with heady aromas and enchanting flavors. Sweet dried fruit and tomatoes are a great contrast to the lamb's gaminess, while chickpeas add hearty texture.

¾ pound cubed lamb shoulder, trimmed of fat

1 teaspoon ground coriander

½ teaspoon ground cumin

½ teaspoon salt

¼ teaspoon ground cinnamon

⅛ teaspoon freshly ground black pepper

1 cup sliced fennel

1 carrot, sliced

2 garlic cloves, minced

1 (15-ounce) can chickpeas, rinsed and drained

½ cup golden raisins

1 large tomato, seeded and chopped

1½ cups Chicken Stock (page 28)

1. In a medium bowl, sprinkle the lamb shoulder with the coriander, cumin, salt, cinnamon, and pepper, and rub the spices into the meat.

2. In the slow cooker, combine the lamb with the remaining ingredients and stir.

3. Cover and cook on low for 8 hours, or until the lamb is very tender.

4. Ladle the stew into 2 bowls and serve.

PER SERVING Calories: 699; Total fat: 23g; Saturated fat: 8g; Cholesterol: 148mg; Carbohydrates: 69g; Fiber: 11g; Protein: 55g

FOUR

BEEF, LAMB & PORK

One of the great things about the long cook times at low heat is that in addition to getting delicious dishes with deep, complex flavors, you must use inexpensive cuts of meat, which typically have the abundance of connective tissue needed in slow cooking. Those connective tissues dissolve during cook time and are responsible for that melt-in-your-mouth richness beef, lamb, and pork are known for. Delicious, effortless meals at a low price.

MUSHROOM-SMOTHERED STEAK

PREP
15 MINUTES

COOK
8½ HOURS
ON LOW

NUT-FREE

SERVES 2

Tender chunks of beef and toothsome mushrooms in a rich creamy sauce make this a comfort food you'll be craving all day. Serve it over mashed potatoes, cooked pasta, or warm brown rice for a deeply satisfying meal.

1 pound chuck eye roast, trimmed of excess fat

2 tablespoons all-purpose flour, divided

½ teaspoon dried marjoram leaves

½ teaspoon salt

⅛ teaspoon freshly ground black pepper

2 tablespoons extra-virgin olive oil

1 cup sliced cremini mushrooms

1 cup sliced button mushrooms

1 cup sliced shiitake mushrooms

1 onion, chopped

2 garlic cloves, minced

1½ cups Beef Stock (page 29)

1 tablespoon soy sauce

½ cup sour cream

1. On a platter, sprinkle the beef with 1 tablespoon of flour and the marjoram, salt, and pepper.

2. In a large skillet over medium heat, heat the oil. Add the beef and brown, turning once, about 5 minutes total.

3. In the bottom of the slow cooker, combine the cremini mushrooms, button mushrooms, shiitake mushrooms, onion, and garlic. Add the steak and top with the stock and soy sauce.

4. Cover and cook on low for 8 hours.

5. In a medium bowl, whisk the sour cream and the remaining 1 tablespoon of flour together with 1 cup of liquid from the slow cooker until well blended. Add the mixture to the slow cooker and stir.

6. Cover and cook on low for 20 to 30 minutes more, until the sauce is thickened, and serve.

PER SERVING Calories: 463; Total fat: 30g; Saturated fat: 11g; Cholesterol: 68mg; Carbohydrates: 28g; Fiber: 4g; Protein: 23g

PREP
20 MINUTES

COOK
10 MINUTES
ON THE
STOVE TOP
plus
7 HOURS
ON LOW

SOY-FREE

NUT-FREE

SPANISH OLIVE MEATLOAF

SERVES 2

Everyone has their favorite meatloaf recipe, but it's fun to mix things up from time to time and try something new. Savory and tender—and delicious—this international version is just the ticket.

1 tablespoon butter	½ teaspoon dried marjoram leaves
1 onion, finely chopped	¼ teaspoon salt
2 garlic cloves, minced	¼ cup chopped green olives
1 egg	1 pound extra-lean ground beef
⅓ cup soft bread crumbs	⅓ cup tomato sauce
½ teaspoon sweet paprika	1 tablespoon Dijon mustard

1. In a small skillet over medium heat, melt the butter. Add the onion and garlic, and sauté, stirring, until tender, about 6 minutes. Remove to a large bowl to cool for 15 minutes.

2. Add the egg, bread crumbs, paprika, marjoram, salt, and olives to the onion mixture and mix well.

3. Add the ground beef to the onion mixture and mix gently but thoroughly, using your hands.

4. Tear off 2 (18-inch-long) strips of heavy-duty aluminum foil. Fold each in half lengthwise twice. Place the foil pieces in the bottom of the slow cooker in an "X."

5. Form the meat mixture into a loaf and place it in the middle of the aluminum foil.

6. In a small bowl, mix the tomato sauce and mustard. Spoon the mixture over the loaf.

7. Cover and cook on low for 6 to 7 hours, or until the meatloaf registers 165°F on a meat thermometer.

8. Using the foil strips as a sling, remove the meatloaf from the slow cooker to a platter. Cover with foil and let stand for 5 minutes.

9. Slice and serve.

PER SERVING Calories: 468; Total fat: 21g; Saturated fat: 9g; Cholesterol: 218mg; Carbohydrates: 17g; Fiber: 4g; Protein: 54g

DID YOU KNOW? Extra-lean ground beef has no more than 5 percent fat, but that's measured by weight, not by calories from fat. That means that in terms of calories, 1 pound of extra-lean ground beef actually contains 23 grams of fat, or 30 percent calories from fat. Still, you must use this type of ground beef when making meatloaf in the slow cooker or the result will be too greasy.

PORK GOULASH

PREP
20 MINUTES

COOK
8½ HOURS
ON LOW

GLUTEN-FREE

SOY-FREE

NUT-FREE

SERVES 2

This pork goulash is a rich and comforting recipe full of succulent pork, tender onion, and tart sauerkraut. If you'd like to decrease the dish's saltiness, rinse and drain the sauerkraut before adding it to the slow cooker.

1 pound pork loin roast, cubed

2 teaspoons sweet paprika

½ teaspoon salt

⅛ teaspoon freshly ground black pepper

1 onion, chopped

2 garlic cloves

2 cups sauerkraut, drained

1 teaspoon caraway seeds

1 cup Chicken Stock (page 28)

½ cup sour cream

1 tablespoon cornstarch

3 slices crisply cooked bacon

1. In a medium bowl, sprinkle the pork with the paprika, salt, and pepper, and rub the spices into the meat.

2. In the bottom of the slow cooker, combine the onion, garlic, sauerkraut, and caraway seeds. Top with the pork, and pour the stock over everything.

3. Cover and cook on low for 8 hours, until the pork is tender.

4. In a small bowl, stir the sour cream together with the cornstarch until well combined. Add ½ cup of hot liquid from the slow cooker and mix with a wire whisk. Stir the mixture into the slow cooker.

5. Cover and cook on low for 20 minutes more, or until thickened. Top with bacon, if desired.

6. Serve topped with the bacon.

PER SERVING Calories: 732; Total fat: 39g; Saturated fat: 17g; Cholesterol: 219mg; Carbohydrates: 21g; Fiber: 7g; Protein: 73g

PREP
20 MINUTES

COOK
13 MINUTES
ON THE
STOVE TOP
plus
5 HOURS
ON LOW

GLUTEN-FREE

SOY-FREE

NUT-FREE

BEEF RISOTTO

SERVES 2

Purists may squirm at the thought of cooking risotto in the slow cooker, but not only does it work, this method is much easier. Who has time these days to stir constantly for 30 minutes? More important, the results of this method are just as delicious.

½ pound lean ground beef

1½ cups Arborio rice

1 onion, chopped

2 garlic cloves, minced

¼ cup dry white wine

4 cups Beef Stock (page 29)

½ teaspoon salt

⅛ teaspoon freshly ground black pepper

½ cup grated Parmesan cheese

1 tablespoon butter

1. In a medium skillet over medium heat, cook the ground beef, stirring to break up the meat, until browned, about 10 minutes. Add the rice and cook for 2 to 3 minutes, stirring constantly, until the rice is toasted. Drain off excess fat.

2. In the slow cooker, combine the beef mixture, onion, and garlic. Add the wine, stock, salt, and pepper and stir well.

3. Cover and cook on low for 5 hours.

4. Stir in the cheese and butter, let stand for 5 minutes, and serve.

PER SERVING Calories: 951; Total fat: 21g; Saturated fat: 11g; Cholesterol: 137mg; Carbohydrates: 122g; Fiber: 5g; Protein: 59g

DID YOU KNOW? Arborio rice is a short-grain rice that releases starch as it cooks. The starch thickens the liquid because it is a branched type of starch called amylopectin. Long-grain rice will not work in this recipe, because the starch it contains is straight, so it won't thicken the liquid.

BBQ RIBS

SERVES 2

PREP
15 MINUTES

COOK
10 MINUTES
IN THE
BROILER
plus
8 HOURS
ON LOW

GLUTEN-FREE

SOY-FREE

NUT-FREE

Brown your pork ribs before adding them to the slow cooker, or the recipe will have too much fat and will cook too quickly. You can use your favorite barbecue sauce in this recipe, but try the one here, from chapter 2.

2 pounds pork baby back ribs

1 tablespoon All-American Dry Rub (page 23)

2 onions, sliced

2 cups baby carrots

1 cup BBQ Sauce (page 40)

1. Preheat the broiler.

2. Sprinkle the ribs with the dry rub and rub it into the meat.

3. Place the ribs on a broiler rack and broil 6 inches from the heat source for 5 minutes, and then turn and broil on the second side until the ribs are brown, about 5 minutes more. Drain off any fat.

4. In the bottom of the slow cooker, combine the onions and baby carrots and top with the ribs.

5. Pour the barbecue sauce over everything.

6. Cover and cook on low for 7 to 8 hours, or until the ribs are very tender, and serve.

PER SERVING Calories: 1341; Total fat: 109g; Saturated fat: 40g; Cholesterol: 361mg; Carbohydrates: 13g; Fiber: 3g; Protein: 74g

PREP
20 MINUTES

COOK
9 HOURS
ON LOW

SOY-FREE

NUT-FREE

BEEF BURGUNDY

SERVES 2

The secret to this rich and elegant main dish is Burgundy wine from the eponymous region in eastern France (you can also buy generic Burgundy from California that is very good). The complex wine-infused stew with chunks of tender meat and earthy mushrooms tastes its best when you use a good wine. A good rule of thumb is if you like drinking the wine, use it in this dish.

¼ cup all-purpose flour

½ teaspoon salt

⅛ teaspoon freshly ground black pepper

1 pound chuck eye roast or sirloin tip, cut into 1½-inch pieces

2 carrots, sliced on the diagonal

1 onion, cut into eight wedges

1 cup sliced cremini mushrooms

1 garlic clove

1 bay leaf

½ teaspoon dried marjoram leaves

1 cup Beef Stock (page 29)

1 cup water

½ cup Burgundy wine

1. On a platter, stir together the flour, salt, and pepper. Add the meat and toss to coat.

2. In the slow cooker, combine the carrots, onion, mushrooms, garlic, bay leaf, and marjoram.

3. Top with the beef, and pour the stock, water, and wine over everything.

4. Cover and cook on low for 8 to 9 hours, or until the beef and vegetables are tender.

5. Remove the bay leaf and serve.

PER SERVING Calories: 267; Total fat: 4g; Saturated fat: 2g; Cholesterol: 43mg; Carbohydrates: 27g; Fiber: 4g; Protein: 19g

PREP IT RIGHT When preparing beef cuts for the slow cooker, it's important to remove excess fat wider than ⅛ inch. Too much fat makes the food taste greasy and also makes it more likely to overcook.

TUSCAN POT ROAST

SERVES 2

PREP
20 MINUTES

COOK
6 MINUTES
ON THE
STOVE TOP
plus
9 HOURS
ON LOW

GLUTEN-FREE

SOY-FREE

NUT-FREE

Melt-in-your-mouth beef, savory portobello mushrooms, silky red wine, and aromatic herbs combine to create an extraordinary taste that's reminiscent of the Tuscan wine country. This pot roast is a flavorful, tender dish, perfect for a chilly evening.

2 tablespoons extra-virgin olive oil

1½ pounds bottom round pot roast

1 onion, chopped

2 garlic cloves, minced

2 carrots, sliced

1 cup sliced portobello mushrooms

2 large tomatoes, seeded and chopped

2 tablespoons chopped fresh celery leaves

2 tablespoons tomato paste

½ cup dry red wine

½ cup Beef Stock (page 29)

½ teaspoon salt

½ teaspoon dried oregano

2 teaspoons minced fresh rosemary leaves

1. In a large skillet over medium heat, heat the oil. Add the roast and brown on both sides, turning once, about 6 minutes total. Remove from the heat.

2. In the slow cooker, combine the onion, garlic, carrots, mushrooms, tomatoes, and celery leaves. Place the roast on top.

3. In a small bowl, stir together the tomato paste, wine, stock, salt, and oregano, mixing well. Pour the mixture over the roast.

4. Cover and cook on low for 8 to 9 hours, or until the beef is very tender.

5. Stir in the fresh rosemary and serve.

PER SERVING Calories: 813; Total fat: 43g; Saturated fat: 12g; Cholesterol: 162mg; Carbohydrates: 30g; Fiber: 6g; Protein: 62g

NEXT DAY Pot roast makes excellent sandwiches the next day. Slice it fairly thick and make sandwiches with some crusty French bread or ciabatta rolls. Add some mayonnaise, mustard, thickly sliced tomato, butter lettuce, and sliced cheese for a delicious lunch.

PREP
15 MINUTES

COOK
8 MINUTES
ON THE
STOVE TOP
plus
8 HOURS
ON LOW

SOY-FREE
———

NUT-FREE
———

BRAISED SHORT RIBS

SERVES 2

As their name suggests, short ribs are shorter than spare ribs. They must be browned first, to remove excess fat and develop flavor, then braised. They're simply succulent after slow cooking, and make a dynamite pasta sauce that's chunky and meaty.

¼ cup all-purpose flour

1 tablespoon All-American Dry Rub (page 23)

2 pounds bone-in beef short ribs

2 tablespoons extra-virgin olive oil

1 cup Beef Stock (page 29)

1 onion, chopped

3 garlic cloves, sliced

2 carrots, sliced

3 tablespoons tomato paste

3 tablespoons ketchup

1 tablespoon Dijon mustard

1 tablespoon honey

1 tablespoon Worcestershire sauce

½ teaspoon dried marjoram leaves

⅛ teaspoon freshly ground black pepper

1. On a platter, mix the flour and dry rub together. Dredge the ribs in the mixture.

2. In a large skillet over medium heat, heat the oil. Add the ribs and brown on both sides, turning once, about 8 minutes total.

3. Remove the ribs from the skillet. Add the beef stock to the skillet and bring to a simmer, scraping up the pan drippings. Remove from the heat.

4. In the slow cooker, combine the onion, garlic, carrots, and ribs on top.

5. Stir the tomato paste, ketchup, mustard, honey, Worcestershire sauce, marjoram, and pepper into the mixture in the skillet, and pour the mixture over the ribs in the slow cooker.

6. Cover and cook on low for 8 hours, or until the ribs are very tender, and serve.

PER SERVING Calories: 1346; Total fat: 92g; Saturated fat: 39g; Cholesterol: 364mg; Carbohydrates: 47g; Fiber: 5g; Protein: 87g

PREP
20 MINUTES

COOK
5 MINUTES
ON THE
STOVE TOP
plus
7 HOURS
ON LOW

SOY-FREE

NUT-FREE

SPICY VEGGIE MEATLOAF

SERVES 2

Great for a weekday meal, this healthy meatloaf filled with veggies and spicy peppers will perk you up after a long day. Serve this dish with a fruit salad and some toasted bread spread with butter.

1 tablespoon extra-virgin olive oil

1 onion, finely chopped

1 red bell pepper, chopped

½ cup chopped button mushrooms

2 garlic cloves, minced

1 jalapeño pepper, minced

⅔ cup soft bread crumbs

1 egg

2 teaspoons chili powder

½ teaspoon salt

¼ teaspoon crushed red pepper flakes

½ pound lean ground beef

⅓ pound ground spicy pork sausage

¼ pound ground lamb

½ cup shredded pepper Jack cheese

1. In a medium skillet over medium heat, heat the olive oil. Add the onion, bell pepper, mushrooms, and garlic and sauté, stirring, until the vegetables are tender, about 5 minutes. Remove to a large bowl and cool for 10 minutes.

2. Add the jalapeño pepper, bread crumbs, egg, chili powder, salt, and red pepper flakes to the vegetable mixture and stir.

3. Add the ground beef, sausage, lamb, and cheese, and mix gently but thoroughly.

4. Tear off 2 (18-inch-long) strips of heavy-duty foil. Fold each in half lengthwise twice. Place the 2 pieces in the bottom of the slow cooker, making an "X."

5. Form the meat mixture into a loaf and place it on top of the foil sling.

6. Cover and cook on low for 6 to 7 hours, or until a meat thermometer registers 165°F.

7. Using the foil sling, remove the meatloaf from the slow cooker to a platter, cover with foil, and let stand for 10 minutes.

8. Slice and serve.

PER SERVING Calories: 730; Total fat: 41g; Saturated fat: 14g; Cholesterol: 290mg; Carbohydrates: 19g; Fiber: 4g; Protein: 69g

PREP
20 MINUTES

COOK
10 MINUTES
ON THE
STOVE TOP
plus
7 HOURS
ON LOW

SOY-FREE

NUT-FREE

THREE-MEAT LASAGNA

SERVES 2

Lasagna is fun to make in the slow cooker. Make sure to use no-cook noodles, which have been parboiled and dried. You can find them at most major grocery stores, or they are easy to order online.

⅓ pound lean ground beef

⅓ pound pork sausage

¼ pound ground dark-meat turkey

1 small onion, chopped

2 garlic cloves, minced

1 (14-ounce) can diced tomatoes, undrained

1 (8-ounce) can tomato sauce

½ cup water

½ teaspoon salt

½ teaspoon dried oregano

½ teaspoon dried basil

⅛ teaspoon freshly ground black pepper

1 cup ricotta cheese

1 (3-ounce) package cream cheese, at room temperature

1 egg

1½ cups shredded mozzarella cheese

6 no-boil lasagna noodles, divided

¼ cup grated Parmesan cheese

1. In a medium skillet over medium heat, cook the beef, sausage, turkey, onion, and garlic, stirring to break up the meat, until the meat is browned, about 10 minutes. Drain well.

2. Add the tomatoes, tomato sauce, water, salt, oregano, basil, and pepper and remove from the heat.

3. In a medium bowl, stir together the ricotta, cream cheese, egg, and mozzarella cheese, mixing well.

4. In the bottom of the slow cooker, layer one-third of the meat sauce. Top the sauce with half the noodles, breaking to fit if necessary. Top the noodles with half the ricotta mixture. Repeat the layers, ending with meat sauce, and sprinkle with the Parmesan cheese.

5. Cover and cook on low for 6 to 7 hours, or until the noodles are tender, and serve.

PER SERVING Calories: 1373; Total fat: 74g; Saturated fat: 36g; Cholesterol: 424mg; Carbohydrates: 63g; Fiber: 5g; Protein: 116g

TERIYAKI PORK ROAST

SERVES 2

PREP
15 MINUTES

COOK
7 HOURS
ON LOW
plus
15 MINUTES
ON HIGH

GLUTEN-FREE

NUT-FREE

Roast pork tastes delicious when cooked using the ingredients in a traditional Japanese teriyaki. For the slow cooker version, choose a pork loin roast or a pork shoulder roast, trimmed of excess fat.

1½ pounds boneless pork roast

2 garlic cloves, cut into slivers

¼ cup honey

1 onion, sliced

¼ cup orange juice

2 tablespoons low-sodium soy sauce

1 tablespoon teriyaki sauce

3 tablespoons brown sugar

2 teaspoons grated fresh ginger

⅛ teaspoon freshly ground black pepper

2 tablespoons water

1 tablespoon cornstarch

1. Using a sharp knife, poke about a dozen holes in the pork roast. Insert the garlic slivers into the holes. Drizzle the roast with the honey and rub it in.

2. In the slow cooker, put the roast on top of the onion.

3. In a small bowl, mix the orange juice, soy sauce, teriyaki sauce, sugar, ginger, and pepper and pour the mixture over the roast.

4. Cover and cook on low for 6 to 7 hours, or until the roast is very tender. Remove the roast and onion from the slow cooker to a platter and cover.

5. In a small bowl, mix the water and cornstarch well. Stir the mixture into the liquid in the slow cooker and turn the heat to high. Cook for 10 to 15 minutes, until thickened.

6. Serve the sauce with the pork and onion.

PER SERVING Calories: 742; Total fat: 12g; Saturated fat: 4g; Cholesterol: 248mg; Carbohydrates: 65g; Fiber: 2g; Protein: 92g

NEXT DAY Use the leftovers to make fried rice. Cook a cup of rice in some chicken stock until tender. Stir-fry a chopped onion, some garlic, and a bell pepper in a bit of oil. Stir in the rice and chopped leftover pork, along with soy sauce to taste, and enjoy.

PREP
15 MINUTES

COOK
9 HOURS
ON LOW

GLUTEN-FREE
———

SOY-FREE
———

NUT-FREE
———

LAMB MARSALA

SERVES 2

This recipe calls for lamb shanks, which you may need to order from the butcher, although most large grocery stores carry them. The shank has a large bone, which adds a velvety texture to the sauce in this elegant recipe. Serve with hot cooked noodles to soak up the wonderful sauce.

2 tablespoons extra-virgin olive oil

2 lamb shanks, trimmed and cracked

½ teaspoon salt

⅛ teaspoon freshly ground black pepper

½ cup Chicken Stock (page 28)

1 leek, white part only, chopped

2 carrots, sliced

2 garlic cloves, minced

1 (14-ounce) can diced tomatoes, undrained

1 cup Marsala wine

2 teaspoons minced fresh rosemary leaves

1. In a large saucepan over medium heat, heat the oil.

2. Sprinkle the lamb with the salt and pepper, add it to the pan, and brown it on all sides, turning several times, about 5 minutes.

3. Remove the lamb from the saucepan to a platter, and add the stock to the pan. Bring the stock to a simmer, scraping up the pan drippings. Remove from the heat.

4. In the slow cooker, combine the leek, carrots, garlic, and tomatoes. Top with the lamb shanks, and pour the stock mixture from the saucepan over everything.

5. Add the wine and rosemary to the slow cooker.

6. Cover and cook on low for 8 to 9 hours, or until the lamb is very tender, and serve.

PER SERVING Calories: 635; Total fat: 27g; Saturated fat: 7g; Cholesterol: 153mg; Carbohydrates: 25g; Fiber: 5g; Protein: 51g

DID YOU KNOW? When a butcher "cracks" lamb shanks, he simply cuts through the bone, exposing the marrow. This melts during cooking to add wonderful rich taste and a velvety texture to the dish. Most shanks are sold already cracked; ask when you purchase them.

CARNITAS

PREP
15 MINUTES

COOK
8 HOURS
ON LOW

GLUTEN-FREE

SOY-FREE

NUT-FREE

SERVES 2

Fill your tacos, enchiladas, and burritos with this spicy, silky shredded pork. Carnitas are usually simmered in lard, but this recipe calls for the healthier chicken stock.

1 pound boneless pork shoulder or loin roast

2 teaspoons chili powder

½ teaspoon dried oregano leaves

½ teaspoon salt

⅛ teaspoon freshly ground black pepper

⅛ teaspoon crushed red pepper flakes

1 onion, chopped

2 garlic cloves, minced

1 jalapeño pepper, minced

½ cup Chicken Stock (page 28)

1. On a platter, sprinkle the pork with the chili powder, oregano, salt, pepper, and crushed red pepper flakes, and rub the spices into the meat.

2. In the slow cooker, combine the onion, garlic, and jalapeño pepper. Top with the pork, and pour the stock over everything.

3. Cover and cook on low for 8 hours, or until the meat is very tender.

4. Remove the meat from the slow cooker and shred.

5. Stir the meat back into the slow cooker and serve.

PER SERVING Calories: 365; Total fat: 9g; Saturated fat: 3g; Cholesterol: 166mg; Carbohydrates: 8g; Fiber: 3g; Protein: 61g

NEXT DAY While carnitas are delicious served straight out of the slow cooker, they are really at their peak the next day. Store the pork in the fridge overnight. When you're ready to eat, heat a tablespoon of oil in a medium skillet. Add the pork and cook until some of the pork is crisp and brown and it's all hot. Serve in tacos with refried beans, tomatoes, and cheese.

CUBAN PORK AND BLACK BEANS

SERVES 2

Salsa, jalapeño pepper, smoked paprika, and cayenne pepper spice up this classic dish that is full of flavor and is just delicious served over hot cooked rice. Chopped tomatoes, serrano pepper, and fresh cilantro punch it up to a great finish. Serve with a fruit or cucumber salad on the side.

1 pound boneless pork shoulder, trimmed

2 teaspoons chili powder

1 teaspoon smoked paprika

½ teaspoon dried oregano leaves

½ teaspoon ground coriander

½ teaspoon salt

⅛ teaspoon ground cayenne pepper

1 onion, chopped

1 red bell pepper, chopped

2 garlic cloves, minced

1 jalapeño pepper, minced

1 (14-ounce) can black beans, rinsed and drained

1 cup Chicken Stock (page 28)

½ cup Red Salsa (page 41)

2 tablespoons freshly squeezed lemon juice

1 tomato, chopped

1 serrano pepper, minced

3 tablespoons minced fresh cilantro

1. On a platter, sprinkle the pork with the chili powder, paprika, oregano, coriander, salt, and cayenne pepper, and rub the spices into the meat.

2. In the slow cooker, combine the onion, red bell pepper, garlic, and jalapeño pepper. Top with the meat.

3. Top the meat with the black beans, stock, salsa, and lemon juice.

4. Cover and cook on low for 7½ to 8 hours, or until the pork is very tender.

5. Remove the pork from the slow cooker and shred. Return the pork to the slow cooker and stir.

6. In a small bowl, mix the tomato, serrano pepper, and cilantro.

7. Serve the pork mixture over rice, topped with the tomato mixture.

PER SERVING Calories: 679; Total fat: 11g; Saturated fat: 3g; Cholesterol: 166mg; Carbohydrates: 66g; Fiber: 23g; Protein: 81g

PREP
20 MINUTES

COOK
8 HOURS
ON LOW

GLUTEN-FREE

SOY-FREE

NUT-FREE

BEEF FAJITAS

SERVES 2

Fajitas are usually grilled using a more expensive cut of meat than the chuck roast used here. Not only will using a much less expensive cut save you money, the meat will be mouth wateringly falling-apart tender.

1¼ pounds boneless beef chuck roast

2 teaspoons chili powder

½ teaspoon ground cumin

½ teaspoon salt

⅛ teaspoon ground cayenne pepper

1 onion, sliced

3 garlic cloves, sliced

1 jalapeño or serrano pepper, minced

1 red bell pepper, sliced

1 yellow bell pepper, sliced

2 tomatoes, seeded and chopped

½ cup Red Salsa (page 41)

1. On a platter, sprinkle the roast with the chili powder, cumin, salt, and cayenne pepper, and rub the spices into the meat.

2. In the slow cooker, top the onion with the meat. Add the garlic, jalapeño pepper, red and yellow bell peppers, and tomatoes. Spoon the salsa over everything.

3. Cover and cook on low for 8 hours, or until the meat is very tender.

4. Remove the meat from the slow cooker and shred.

5. Return the meat to the slow cooker, stir, and serve.

PER SERVING Calories: 643; Total fat: 19g; Saturated fat: 7g; Cholesterol: 253mg; Carbohydrates: 25g; Fiber: 7g; Protein: 91g

PERFECT PAIR Serve this delicious recipe with warmed flour or corn tortillas, sour cream, guacamole, chopped fresh tomatoes, cilantro, and sliced pickled jalapeño peppers for a true Mexican feast. A bottle of cold beer makes a wonderful complement.

RED CURRY BEEF

SERVES 2

PREP
15 MINUTES

COOK
8 HOURS
ON LOW

GLUTEN-FREE

NUT-FREE

This classic Thai dish uses ingredients that are easy to find at any grocery store. The curry paste is essential to this recipe because it provides heat and depth of flavor. Serve over hot cooked rice with a cool green salad.

1 pound beef chuck eye roast, cut into 1½-inch cubes

2 teaspoons Curry Rub (page 23)

1 tablespoon brown sugar

½ teaspoon lime zest

⅛ teaspoon freshly ground black pepper

1 onion, chopped

4 garlic cloves, minced

1½ tablespoons red curry paste

2 tablespoons freshly squeezed lime juice

1 tablespoon honey

2 teaspoons grated fresh ginger

1 cup coconut milk

½ cup Beef Stock (page 29)

1 tablespoon fish sauce

2 tablespoons chopped cilantro

1. On a platter, sprinkle the beef with the curry rub, brown sugar, lime zest, and pepper, and rub the spices into the meat.

2. In the slow cooker, combine the onion and garlic. Top with the meat.

3. In a medium bowl, mix the red curry paste, lime juice, honey, ginger, coconut milk, stock, and fish sauce until well combined. Pour the mixture into the slow cooker.

4. Cover and cook on low for 8 hours, or until the beef is very tender.

5. Garnish with the cilantro and serve.

PER SERVING Calories: 524; Total fat: 36g; Saturated fat: 28g; Cholesterol: 43mg; Carbohydrates: 36g; Fiber: 5g; Protein: 20g

SHREDDED SPICY BEEF SANDWICHES

SERVES 2

This beef mixture is delicious in sandwiches, whether you use hamburger buns, crusty rolls, or pita breads. If you don't use the BBQ Sauce recipe from this book, use your own homemade barbecue sauce or look for one in the grocery store that does not use high-fructose corn syrup (HFCS), a cheap substitute for sugar.

1 onion, chopped

4 garlic cloves, minced

2 jalapeño peppers, minced

1½ pounds boneless beef chuck roast

½ cup BBQ Sauce (page 40)

2 tablespoons honey

2 tablespoons Dijon mustard

½ teaspoon salt

⅛ teaspoon ground cayenne pepper

2 or 3 split, toasted ciabatta buns

½ cup torn butter lettuce

1. In the bottom of the slow cooker, combine the onion, garlic, and jalapeño peppers. Top with the beef.

2. In a small bowl, mix the barbecue sauce, honey, mustard, salt, and cayenne pepper, and pour the mixture over the beef.

3. Cover and cook on low for 8 hours.

4. Remove the beef and shred. Return the beef to the slow cooker and stir.

5. Make sandwiches with the buns and lettuce and serve.

PER SERVING Calories: 1045; Total fat: 25g; Saturated fat: 9g; Cholesterol: 304mg; Carbohydrates: 87g; Fiber: 5g; Protein: 114g

NEXT DAY Use this recipe to make fabulous enchiladas or tacos. Just warm the beef mixture and combine it with some refried beans and shredded cheese. Roll the mixture up in flour tortillas and bake until warm, or fill warmed taco shells with the beef.

KIMCHI PULLED PORK

SERVES 2

Kimchi (or kimchee), a fermented spicy-sour Korean condiment made from cabbage, radishes, garlic, and onions along with peppers and spices, is delicious mixed into pulled pork. The kimchi will mellow a bit after a long cooking time, but it will still have lots of flavor.

2 tablespoons low-sodium soy sauce

2 tablespoons brown sugar

2 teaspoons minced fresh ginger

2 garlic cloves, minced

⅛ teaspoon freshly ground black pepper

1½ pounds boneless pork shoulder roast, excess fat trimmed

1½ cups kimchi

¼ cup Chicken Stock (page 28)

1. In a small bowl, mix the soy sauce, brown sugar, ginger, garlic, and pepper.

2. In the slow cooker, spread the mixture over the roast.

3. Pour the kimchi and stock over the roast.

4. Cover and cook on low for 8 hours.

5. Remove the pork from the slow cooker and shred.

6. Return the meat to the slow cooker, stir, and serve.

PER SERVING Calories: 939; Total fat: 68g; Saturated fat: 24g; Cholesterol: 241mg; Carbohydrates: 14g; Fiber: 0g; Protein: 59g

FIVE

POULTRY

Chicken, turkey, and Cornish hens are all delicious when cooked in the slow cooker, but there is a caveat. Since newer slow cookers cook at a hotter temperature than those from 10 years ago, we have to be careful with boneless, skinless chicken breasts. That cut will cook in 4 to 5 hours on low in most slow cookers. Use bone-in, skinless chicken breasts to cook for 7 hours; the bone helps shield the meat and keep it tender. From comforting classics to more international recipes, your slow cooker will give you an easy meal you'll want to prepare again and again.

ROTISSERIE CHICKEN

SERVES 2

True rotisserie chickens are roasted on a spit; they turn constantly and are basted while they cook. The slow cooker mimics these cooking methods, so this chicken is incredibly tender, flavorful, and moist. The chicken may fall apart when you remove it from the slow cooker—which just means carving will be easier! Just make sure the chicken you buy will fit in the slow cooker with some room to spare.

Nonstick cooking spray

3 garlic cloves, crushed

1 teaspoon salt

1½ teaspoons ground smoked paprika

1 teaspoon dried thyme leaves

¼ teaspoon freshly ground black pepper

1 (2½- to 3-pound) roasting or broiler chicken

1 lemon

1. Spray the slow cooker with nonstick cooking spray. Tear off 4 (18-inch-long) pieces of foil. Scrunch the foil into balls and place in the slow cooker.

2. In a small bowl, mix the crushed garlic, salt, paprika, thyme, and pepper until well combined. Sprinkle one-quarter of this mixture inside the chicken; rub the rest onto the chicken skin.

3. Roll the lemon on the counter beneath your palm to soften it. Quarter the lemon. Put 2 quarters inside the chicken. Squeeze the remaining 2 quarters over the chicken, and put those pieces in the slow cooker between the foil balls.

continued

4. Place the chicken, breast-side down, on top of the foil balls.

5. Cover and cook on low for 8 hours, or until the chicken registers 165°F on a meat thermometer and is very tender.

6. Carve and serve.

PER SERVING Calories: 1156; Total fat: 46g; Saturated fat: 5g; Cholesterol: 510mg; Carbohydrates: 5g; Fiber: 1g; Protein: 171g

PREP IT RIGHT Do not rinse chicken or turkey before you cook it. This step does not clean the chicken—it spreads bacteria around your kitchen. Under running water, bacteria can aerosolize and contaminate surfaces up to 3 feet away from the faucet. Just pat the chicken dry and use as directed in the recipe.

HERBED TURKEY BREAST

SERVES 2

PREP
10 MINUTES

COOK
10 MINUTES
ON THE
STOVE TOP
plus
9 HOURS
ON LOW

SOY-FREE

GLUTEN-FREE

NUT-FREE

Serve up that turkey, even if it's not Thanksgiving! In fact, this recipe is a great way to make lots of turkey for salads and sandwiches. It can be frozen after it's cooked, too. Use a bone-in turkey breast for best results, and feel free to experiment with your favorite herbs.

1 (2½- to 3-pound) bone-in half turkey breast

3 garlic cloves, cut into slivers

2 tablespoons chopped fresh flat-leaf parsley

2 tablespoons butter, at room temperature

1 teaspoon dried basil

1 teaspoon dried thyme

½ teaspoon dried sage leaves

1 teaspoon salt

⅛ teaspoon freshly ground black pepper

2 onions, sliced

1 cup Chicken Stock (page 28)

1. Using a sharp knife, poke holes in the turkey breast. Push the garlic slivers and the parsley into the holes.

2. On a platter, rub the turkey with the butter and sprinkle it with the basil, thyme, sage, salt, and pepper.

3. In the slow cooker, set the turkey on top of the onions and pour the stock over everything.

4. Cover and cook on low for 8 to 9 hours, or until the turkey registers 160°F on a meat thermometer.

continued

5. Remove the turkey from the slow cooker to a clean platter and cover it with foil; let stand for 10 minutes.

6. In a saucepan over high heat, boil the liquid and onions from the slow cooker until slightly reduced, 6 to 8 minutes.

7. Slice the turkey and serve it with the gravy.

PER SERVING Calories: 602; Total fat: 14g; Saturated fat: 7g; Cholesterol: 312mg; Carbohydrates: 13g; Fiber: 3g; Protein: 115g

DID YOU KNOW? If the turkey breast half comes with the skin attached, leave it on during cooking. The skin adds fat and moisture to the meat as it cooks and helps protect it from the heat. Remove and discard the skin after cooking as it will not have a palatable texture.

LEMON CHICKEN

SERVES 2

PREP
20 MINUTES

COOK
5 MINUTES
ON THE
STOVE TOP
plus
7 HOURS
ON LOW

SOY-FREE

NUT-FREE

Lemon juice, lemon zest, and sliced lemons give this dish its bright, intense flavor as well as its name. Serve it over hot cooked rice or pasta with some green beans and fruit salad.

¼ cup all-purpose flour

½ teaspoon salt

⅛ teaspoon freshly ground black pepper

½ teaspoon lemon zest

½ teaspoon dried thyme leaves

6 bone-in, skin-on chicken thighs

2 tablespoons extra-virgin olive oil

½ cup Chicken Stock (page 28)

3 tablespoons freshly squeezed lemon juice

1 tablespoon honey

2 lemons, sliced and seeded

1 leek, white part only, chopped

3 garlic cloves, minced

1. On a plate, mix the flour, salt, pepper, lemon zest, and thyme. Dredge the chicken thighs in the mixture.

2. In a large skillet over medium heat, heat the oil. Add the chicken thighs, skin-side down, and brown, about 5 minutes. Do not turn over to brown the other side. Remove the chicken from the skillet to a paper towel–lined plate and set aside.

3. In the skillet over medium-low heat, bring the stock to a simmer, stirring to remove the pan drippings. Remove the skillet from the heat. Stir in the lemon juice and honey.

4. In the slow cooker, combine the lemon slices, leek, and garlic. Top with the chicken.

5. Pour the chicken stock mixture over everything.

6. Cover and cook on low for 7 hours, or until the chicken registers 165°F on a meat thermometer, and serve.

PER SERVING Calories: 582; Total fat: 27g; Saturated fat: 5g; Cholesterol: 255mg; Carbohydrates: 29g; Fiber: 2g; Protein: 63g

CHICKEN WITH WHITE WINE AND HERBS

PREP
20 MINUTES

COOK
5 MINUTES
ON THE
STOVE TOP
plus
7 HOURS
ON LOW

SOY-FREE

NUT-FREE

SERVES 2

Bone-in, skin-on chicken thighs produce the most moist, flavorful result, as the bone and skin add flavor and fat and protect the flesh while the meat cooks. Serve this delectable, fragrant dish over hot cooked rice with some fresh herbs stirred in.

7 bone-in, skin-on chicken thighs

2 tablespoons Dijon mustard

1 teaspoon ground paprika

1 teaspoon dried thyme leaves

½ teaspoon dried basil leaves

3 tablespoons all-purpose flour

½ teaspoon salt

⅛ teaspoon freshly ground black pepper

1 tablespoon extra-virgin olive oil

½ cup dry white wine

¼ cup Chicken Stock (page 28)

1. On a platter, loosen the skin from the chicken.

2. In a small bowl, mix the mustard, paprika, thyme, and basil, and rub the mixture onto the chicken meat, beneath the skin. Spread the chicken skin back over this mixture and secure with toothpicks.

3. Sprinkle the chicken with the flour, salt, and pepper.

4. In a medium skillet over medium heat, heat the oil. Add the chicken, skin-side down, and brown, about 4 minutes. Do not turn the chicken over. Remove the chicken from the skillet to the slow cooker.

5. Add the wine and stock to the skillet and bring to a simmer, stirring to remove the pan drippings.

6. Pour the wine mixture over the chicken in the slow cooker.

7. Cover and cook on low for 7 hours, or until the chicken registers 165°F on a meat thermometer.

8. Remove the toothpicks and serve.

PER SERVING Calories: 663; Total fat: 26g; Saturated fat: 6g; Cholesterol: 382mg; Carbohydrates: 12g; Fiber: 1g; Protein: 92g

PREP
15 MINUTES

COOK
7 HOURS
ON LOW

SOY-FREE

NUT-FREE

TURKEY TENDERLOINS WITH RAISIN STUFFING

SERVES 2

Now this is an excellent Thanksgiving dinner alternative for two people. The stuffing is sweet and savory, the turkey moist and tender. Serve with green beans, a green salad tossed with mushrooms and grape tomatoes, and white wine for a lovely meal.

5 slices oatmeal bread, cubed

1 small onion, chopped

2 garlic cloves, minced

½ cup raisins

1 egg

2 tablespoons butter, melted

½ teaspoon salt

⅛ teaspoon freshly ground black pepper

½ cup Chicken Stock (page 28)

2 (1-pound) turkey tenderloins

2 tablespoons Dijon mustard

2 tablespoons honey

1 teaspoon poultry seasoning

1. In the slow cooker, combine the bread, onion, garlic, raisins, egg, butter, salt, and pepper, and mix. Drizzle the stock over everything and stir gently to coat.

2. On a platter, rub the turkey tenderloins with the Dijon mustard and honey, and then sprinkle with the poultry seasoning. Place the tenderloins over the bread mixture in the slow cooker.

3. Cover and cook on low for 6 to 7 hours, until the turkey registers 160°F on a meat thermometer.

4. Slice the turkey and serve it with the stuffing.

PER SERVING Calories: 1121; Total fat: 25g; Saturated fat: 9g; Cholesterol: 293mg; Carbohydrates: 104g; Fiber: 5g; Protein: 128g

NEXT DAY The leftovers from this recipe make a fabulous hot sandwich. Hollow out crusty rolls and add mayonnaise, sliced turkey, and the stuffing. Wrap in foil and bake at 350°F for 15 to 20 minutes, until hot.

CORNISH HENS AND VEGGIES

SERVES 2

Chunky potatoes, sweet carrots, and tender mushrooms round out these cooked-to-perfection Cornish hens, making this one-pot meal an elegant choice for a weekend. Fruit salad would make an excellent dessert.

2 Cornish hens

½ teaspoon salt

½ teaspoon poultry seasoning

⅛ teaspoon freshly ground black pepper

1 small lemon, cut into eighths

1 cup sliced cremini mushrooms

2 carrots, sliced

1 onion, chopped

2 garlic cloves, minced

2 Yukon Gold potatoes, cubed

½ cup Chicken Stock (page 28)

1. On a platter, sprinkle the hens with the salt, poultry seasoning, and pepper. Stuff the lemon slices into the hens' cavities and set aside.

2. In the slow cooker, combine the mushrooms, carrots, onion, garlic, and potatoes. Top with the hens and pour the stock over everything.

3. Cover and cook on low for 8 hours, or until the hens register 165°F on a meat thermometer.

4. Serve the hens with the vegetables.

PER SERVING Calories: 497; Total fat: 9g; Saturated fat: 2g; Cholesterol: 233mg; Carbohydrates: 47g; Fiber: 6g; Protein: 58g

PERFECT PAIR Serve this sophisticated recipe with a green salad tossed with fresh chopped tomatoes or cherry tomatoes and cubed avocado. Crusty dinner rolls will soak up the delicious sauce.

PREP
15 MINUTES

COOK
7 HOURS
ON LOW

SOY-FREE

NUT-FREE

CHICKEN PRIMAVERA SANDWICHES

SERVES 2

While primavera is usually prepared in Italy as a pasta dish with fresh veggies, here we pile succulent chicken along with colorful vegetables on a toasted crusty roll for a wonderful sandwich. Make this recipe your own by selecting your favorite vegetables.

1 onion, sliced

2 garlic cloves, sliced

1 carrot, slivered

1 red bell pepper, chopped

5 boneless, skinless chicken thighs

½ teaspoon salt

½ teaspoon dried thyme leaves

⅛ teaspoon freshly ground black pepper

¼ cup Chicken Stock (page 28)

2 crusty sandwich rolls, split and toasted

2 tablespoons mayonnaise

2 tablespoons grainy mustard

1. In the slow cooker, combine the onion, garlic, carrot, and red bell pepper.

2. On a platter, sprinkle the chicken with the salt, thyme, and pepper, and place the chicken on top of the vegetables in the slow cooker. Pour the stock over everything.

3. Cover and cook on low for 7 hours, or until the chicken registers 165°F on a meat thermometer.

4. Remove the chicken from the slow cooker to a clean platter and shred. Return the meat to the slow cooker and stir.

5. Make sandwiches with the rolls, mayonnaise, and mustard, and serve.

PER SERVING Calories: 749; Total fat: 27g; Saturated fat: 6g; Cholesterol: 253mg; Carbohydrates: 36g; Fiber: 4g; Protein: 87g

PERFECT PAIR This recipe is also delicious served over hot cooked rice or pasta. Or buy rolls of premade polenta, slice them, and sauté until crisp and brown. Serve the rolls with this recipe for a nice change of pace.

CHICKEN-SWEET POTATO SHEPHERD'S PIE

SERVES 2

PREP
20 MINUTES

COOK
25 MINUTES
ON THE
STOVE TOP
plus
7 HOURS
ON LOW

SOY-FREE

NUT-FREE

Hearty shepherd's pie is a classic comfort food. Using mashed sweet potatoes as a topper instead of russet potatoes adds color, nutrition, and a sweet note to this savory mix of meat, vegetables, and luscious gravy.

2 medium sweet potatoes, peeled and cubed

2 tablespoons butter

¼ cup light cream

¾ teaspoon salt, divided

1 leek, white part only, chopped

2 garlic cloves, minced

2 carrots, sliced

2 celery stalks, sliced

5 boneless, skinless chicken thighs, cubed

¼ cup all-purpose flour

½ cup Chicken Stock (page 28)

3 tablespoons tomato paste

½ teaspoon dried thyme leaves

1. In a medium saucepan over high heat, cover the sweet potatoes with water. Bring to a boil, and then reduce the heat to low and simmer for 20 to 25 minutes, or until the potatoes are tender.

2. Drain the potatoes and return them to the hot pot. Add the butter and mash the potatoes. Beat in the cream and ¼ teaspoon of salt and set aside.

3. In the slow cooker, combine the leek, garlic, carrots, and celery.

4. In a medium bowl, toss the chicken thighs with the flour and the remaining ½ teaspoon of salt, and add them to the slow cooker, stirring to combine.

5. In a small bowl, mix the stock, tomato paste, and thyme; pour the mixture into the slow cooker.

6. Spoon the mashed sweet potatoes on top of the chicken mixture.

7. Cover and cook on low for 6 to 7 hours, or until the chicken mixture is bubbly and the chicken registers 165°F on a meat thermometer, and serve.

PER SERVING Calories: 994; Total fat: 38g; Saturated fat: 16g; Cholesterol: 296mg; Carbohydrates: 73g; Fiber: 10g; Protein: 88g

PREP
20 MINUTES

COOK
7 HOURS
ON LOW

SOY-FREE

NUT-FREE

CHICKEN AND CORNBREAD STUFFING

SERVES 2

Chicken with stuffing is a classic slow cooker recipe, but this recipe is a bit different because it uses cornbread and dried fruits instead of regular bread and vegetables. The fruit plumps up a bit as it cooks and adds flavor to this colorful recipe.

Nonstick cooking spray

3 cups cubed cornbread

1 onion, chopped

⅓ cup dried cranberries

⅓ cup golden raisins

3 tablespoons dark raisins

¼ cup whole milk

¼ cup sour cream

¼ cup Chicken Stock (page 28)

2 tablespoons butter, melted

¾ teaspoon salt, divided

½ teaspoon dried sage leaves

⅛ teaspoon freshly ground black pepper

2 boneless, skinless chicken breasts

½ teaspoon ground sweet paprika

1. Spray the slow cooker with the nonstick cooking spray.

2. In the slow cooker, combine the cornbread cubes, onion, cranberries, and golden and dark raisins.

3. In a small bowl, mix the milk, sour cream, stock, butter, ½ teaspoon of salt, sage, and pepper, combining well. Pour this mixture over the stuffing mixture and stir to coat.

4. On a platter, sprinkle the chicken with the paprika and the remaining ¼ teaspoon of salt, and place it on top of the stuffing.

5. Cover and cook on low for 6 to 7 hours, or until the chicken registers 160°F on a meat thermometer, and serve.

PER SERVING Calories: 759; Total fat: 30g; Saturated fat: 15g; Cholesterol: 171mg; Carbohydrates: 72g; Fiber: 4g; Protein: 45g

PERFECT PAIR To make cornbread, in a small bowl, mix 2 tablespoons melted butter, 2 tablespoons oil, ¾ cup milk, ¼ cup sour cream, 1 egg, 1¼ cups cornmeal, 1 cup flour, ⅓ cup sugar, 2 teaspoons baking powder, and ¼ teaspoon salt. Bake in an 8-inch-square pan at 400°F for 20 to 25 minutes.

BUFFALO CHICKEN STROGANOFF

SERVES 2

Made famous by the Anchor Bar in Buffalo, New York, Buffalo wings are coated in a hot, spicy sauce and served with blue cheese dressing and veggies. Here, tasty veggies transform that appetizer into a hearty, delicious main dish.

1 onion, chopped

3 garlic cloves, minced

1 cup sliced cremini mushrooms

3 celery stalks, sliced

1 red bell pepper, sliced

2 tablespoons minced celery leaves

5 boneless, skinless chicken thighs, cubed

3 tablespoons all-purpose flour

½ teaspoon dried marjoram leaves

½ teaspoon salt

⅛ teaspoon freshly ground black pepper

1¼ cups Chicken Stock (page 28)

¼ cup Buffalo wing hot sauce

1 bay leaf

3 ounces cream cheese, cubed

¼ cup sour cream

¼ cup crumbled blue cheese

1. In the slow cooker, combine the onion, garlic, mushrooms, celery, bell pepper, and celery leaves.

2. In a large bowl, toss the chicken thighs with the flour, marjoram, salt, and pepper, and place them on top of the vegetables in the slow cooker.

3. In a small bowl, mix the stock with the hot sauce and bay leaf; pour the mixture into the slow cooker.

4. Cover and cook on low for 7 hours, and then remove and discard the bay leaf.

continued

5. Stir in the cream cheese and sour cream, cover, and cook on low for 20 to 30 minutes more, or until the cream cheese is melted. Gently stir.

6. Stir in the blue cheese and serve.

PER SERVING Calories: 1047; Total fat: 53g; Saturated fat: 24g; Cholesterol: 384mg; Carbohydrates: 25g; Fiber: 4g; Protein: 113g

PERFECT PAIR This delicious recipe can be served over hot cooked rice or pasta, or serve it over toasted and buttered English muffins for a type of chicken à la king. It would also be delicious served over hot mashed sweet potatoes.

TEX-MEX CHICKEN AND RICE

SERVES 2

PREP
20 MINUTES

COOK
7 HOURS
ON LOW

GLUTEN-FREE

SOY-FREE

NUT-FREE

Usually made with beans and lots of vegetables, Tex-Mex cuisine is spicy and fresh. Spicy salsa and nutty long-grain brown rice meld with sweet bell pepper and hot jalapeño for a delicious meal with a kick.

1 onion, chopped

1 red bell pepper, chopped

3 garlic cloves, minced

1 jalapeño pepper, minced

1 (14-ounce) can black beans, rinsed and drained

½ cup long-grain brown rice

5 boneless, skinless chicken thighs, cut into strips

2 teaspoons chili powder

½ teaspoon ground cumin

½ teaspoon dried oregano leaves

½ teaspoon salt

⅛ teaspoon freshly ground black pepper

1 cup Red Salsa (page 41)

1 cup Chicken Stock (page 28)

½ cup shredded pepper Jack cheese

1. In the slow cooker, combine the onion, bell pepper, garlic, jalapeño pepper, black beans, and rice.

2. In a large bowl, toss the chicken with the chili powder, cumin, oregano, salt, and pepper, and place it on top of the bean mixture in the slow cooker.

3. Pour the salsa and stock over everything.

4. Cover and cook on low for 7 hours.

5. Sprinkle with the cheese, let stand for 5 minutes, and then serve.

PER SERVING Calories: 1156; Total fat: 33g; Saturated fat: 12g; Cholesterol: 275mg; Carbohydrates: 102g; Fiber: 25g; Protein: 112g

PREP
5 MINUTES

COOK
7 HOURS
ON LOW
plus
30 MINUTES
ON HIGH

GLUTEN-FREE

SOY-FREE

NUT-FREE

BBQ PULLED CHICKEN SANDWICHES

SERVES 2

This is probably the easiest recipe in the book, once you have the barbecue sauce made. In the slow cooker, the chicken becomes incredibly moist and tender because it's cooked on the bone and with skin. After 7½ hours, the chicken is a snap to shred, and the resulting sandwiches are pure perfection.

6 bone-in, skin-on chicken thighs

1 onion, chopped

2 garlic cloves, minced

1 tablespoon chili powder

1 cup BBQ Sauce (page 40)

2 hamburger buns, split and toasted

1. In the slow cooker, combine all the ingredients except the hamburger buns.

2. Cover and cook on low for 7 hours, or until the chicken registers 165°F on a meat thermometer.

3. Remove the chicken from the slow cooker. Remove the meat from the bones and discard the bones and skin. Shred the chicken and return it to the slow cooker.

4. Leaving the slow cooker uncovered, cook on high for 30 minutes.

5. Make sandwiches with the hamburger buns, and serve.

PER SERVING Calories: 912; Total fat: 51g; Saturated fat: 13g; Cholesterol: 285mg; Carbohydrates: 52g; Fiber: 4g; Protein: 62g

SEASONAL SUBSTITUTION You can use this recipe to make BBQ Beef Sandwiches or BBQ Pork Sandwiches, depending on your mood. Just substitute a 1¼-pound chuck eye roast or a 1¼-pound boneless pork loin roast for the chicken. Add chopped fresh tomatoes when they are in season.

PREP
20 MINUTES

COOK
7 HOURS
ON LOW

GLUTEN-FREE

SOY-FREE

NUT-FREE

CUBAN CHICKEN AND BEANS

SERVES 2

Cuban cuisine is spicy and well rounded. Jerk seasoning is a delicious addition to this spicy dish and adds real depth of flavor. Cubed mango stirred in at the end of cooking time adds a cooling and sweet note.

2 boneless, skinless chicken breasts

2 teaspoons jerk seasoning

½ teaspoon salt

1 onion, chopped

2 garlic cloves, minced

1 serrano pepper, minced

1 (14-ounce) can black beans, rinsed and drained

⅔ cup long-grain brown rice

1⅓ cups Chicken Stock (page 28)

2 tablespoons freshly squeezed lime juice

1 tablespoon honey

1 bay leaf

2 tablespoons minced black olives

1 mango, peeled and cubed

1. On a platter, sprinkle the chicken breasts with the jerk seasoning and salt; set aside.

2. In the slow cooker, combine the onion, garlic, serrano pepper, black beans, and rice.

3. Pour the stock, lime juice, and honey into the slow cooker, and mix. Add the bay leaf.

4. Top with the chicken and sprinkle with the olives.

5. Cover and cook on low for 6 to 7 hours, or until the chicken registers 160°F on a meat thermometer.

6. Remove the chicken from the slow cooker to a clean platter. Remove the bay leaf from the slow cooker and discard.

7. Stir the mango into the mixture in the slow cooker, and serve with the chicken.

PER SERVING Calories: 919; Total fat: 15g; Saturated fat: 3g; Cholesterol: 125mg; Carbohydrates: 135g; Fiber: 24g; Protein: 64g

NEXT DAY If you have some of the bean mixture left over, it is delicious made into quesadillas. Just spread some between two flour or corn tortillas, and add shredded pepper Jack cheese. Heat in a large skillet, turning once, until hot, and then cut into slices and serve.

PREP
10 MINUTES

COOK
8 HOURS
ON LOW

SOY-FREE

NUT-FREE

CHICKEN CACCIATORE

SERVES 2

Cacciatore means "hunter" in Italian, and lucky for you, you'll have no trouble hunting down the ingredients for this palate-pleasing meal. Tangy tomatoes, aromatic herbs, and savory mushrooms in a well-seasoned sauce turn chicken into a rich and rustic main dish perfect for enjoying in front of the fire on a cold night.

5 bone-in, skinless chicken thighs

½ teaspoon dried oregano leaves

½ teaspoon dried basil leaves

½ teaspoon salt

⅛ teaspoon freshly ground black pepper

1 onion, chopped

1 red bell pepper, sliced

1 cup sliced cremini mushrooms

3 garlic cloves, minced

3 tablespoons tomato paste

1 (14-ounce) can diced tomatoes, undrained

1 (8-ounce) can tomato sauce

1. On a platter, sprinkle the chicken with the oregano, basil, salt, and pepper; set aside.

2. In the slow cooker, combine the onion, bell pepper, mushrooms, and garlic. Top with the chicken.

3. In a small bowl, mix the tomato paste, tomatoes, and tomato sauce. Pour the mixture into the slow cooker.

4. Cover and cook on low for 8 hours, or until the chicken registers 160°F on a meat thermometer, and serve.

PER SERVING Calories: 801; Total fat: 41g; Saturated fat: 12g; Cholesterol: 285mg; Carbohydrates: 30g; Fiber: 8g; Protein: 64g

CURRIED CHICKEN THIGHS

SERVES 2

PREP
15 MINUTES

COOK
8 HOURS
ON LOW
plus
15 MINUTES
ON HIGH

GLUTEN-FREE

SOY-FREE

NUT-FREE

Your own Curry Rub (page 23) is perfect in this flavorful, aromatic recipe. Adding sweet potatoes and carrots to this dish makes it a one-dish meal. All you need to serve with this recipe is a green salad tossed with some sliced mushrooms.

1 large sweet potato, peeled and cubed

1 cup sliced button mushrooms

1 cup baby carrots

1 onion, chopped

2 garlic cloves, minced

2 teaspoons grated fresh ginger

5 bone-in, skinless chicken thighs

2 teaspoons Curry Rub (page 23)

½ cup Chicken Stock (page 28)

1 tablespoon cornstarch

¼ cup water

1. In the slow cooker, combine the sweet potato, mushrooms, carrots, onion, garlic, and ginger.

2. On a platter, rub the chicken thighs with the curry rub and place them on top of the vegetables in the slow cooker.

3. Pour the stock over everything.

4. Cover and cook on low for 8 hours.

5. In a small bowl, mix the cornstarch and water. Stir the mixture into the slow cooker.

6. Cover and cook on high for 10 to 15 minutes, or until the sauce is thickened, and serve.

PER SERVING Calories: 478; Total fat: 13g; Saturated fat: 3g; Cholesterol: 255mg; Carbohydrates: 33g; Fiber: 6g; Protein: 64g

PREP
20 MINUTES

COOK
7 HOURS
ON LOW

SOY-FREE

NUT-FREE

FRUIT-STUFFED TURKEY THIGHS

SERVES 2

Turkey thighs are deliciously moist and tender and perfect filled with this sweet and savory fruit-and-bread stuffing. Even better, this is a one-dish meal since the turkey is cooked with potatoes, mushrooms, and carrots. Creamer potatoes are new potatoes with a light yellow skin that you can find in the produce section of the grocery store, often in boxes.

1 skin-on, boneless turkey thigh

½ teaspoon salt

⅛ teaspoon freshly ground black pepper

1 slice raisin bread, cubed

1 garlic clove, minced

2 tablespoons dark raisins

2 tablespoons chopped dried apricots

1 tablespoon water

½ teaspoon dried thyme leaves

½ teaspoon ground sweet paprika

2 teaspoons brown sugar

2 cups creamer potatoes

1 cup baby carrots

1 cup sliced button mushrooms

1 onion, chopped

½ cup Chicken Stock (page 28)

2 tablespoons white wine vinegar

1. Place the turkey thigh on a work surface, skin-side down. Sprinkle with the salt and pepper.

2. In a small bowl, toss together the bread cubes, garlic, raisins, apricots, water, and thyme. Place the mixture on the turkey thigh.

3. Roll the turkey around the stuffing and tie the bundle closed with kitchen twine. Rub the skin with the paprika and brown sugar.

4. In the slow cooker, combine the potatoes, carrots, mushrooms, and onion, and top with the turkey. Pour the stock and vinegar over everything.

5. Cover and cook on low for 7 hours, or until the turkey registers 165°F on a meat thermometer.

6. Remove the turkey from the slow cooker, and remove and discard the string. Slice and serve with the vegetables.

PER SERVING Calories: 494; Total fat: 16g; Saturated fat: 4g; Cholesterol: 60mg; Carbohydrates: 51g; Fiber: 7g; Protein: 37g

SEASONAL SUBSTITUTION You can make this recipe with boneless chicken thighs as well, if you can't find turkey thighs. Use 5 chicken thighs and stuff each with the fruit stuffing. Roll up and secure each with toothpicks, and then cook as directed. One serving would be 2 to 3 thighs.

CHICKEN ENCHILADAS WITH MOLE SAUCE

SERVES 2

PREP
20 MINUTES

COOK
9 HOURS
ON LOW
plus
5 MINUTES
ON THE
STOVE TOP

NUT-FREE

SOY-FREE

These enchiladas are hearty and packed with flavor, from the moist and tender filling, to the mole, to the orange zest and fragrant fresh cilantro. This chicken filling can be used in many different ways. It freezes well, too. It's best to use your own mole sauce, but you can buy it at most larger grocery stores in a pinch.

1 onion, chopped

3 garlic cloves, minced

6 bone-in, skinless chicken thighs

½ teaspoon salt

⅛ teaspoon freshly ground black pepper

1½ cups Mole Sauce (page 35), divided

4 corn tortillas

¼ cup crumbled Cotija cheese

½ teaspoon orange zest

2 tablespoons chopped cilantro

1. In the slow cooker, combine the onion and garlic.

2. On a platter, sprinkle the chicken with the salt and pepper; place it in the slow cooker.

3. Cover the chicken with 1 cup of mole sauce. Keep the remaining ½ cup of mole refrigerated.

4. Cover and cook on low for 9 hours.

5. Remove the chicken from the slow cooker to a clean platter, and remove the meat from the bones; discard the bones. Shred the meat and stir it into the slow cooker.

continued

6. In a small saucepan over medium heat, heat the remaining ½ cup of mole until it bubbles, about 5 minutes.

7. Fill the tortillas with the chicken mixture and roll them up carefully, as corn tortillas tend to break more easily than flour.

8. Top the enchiladas with the hot mole, cheese, orange zest, and cilantro, and serve. You could bake the enchiladas at this point in a greased casserole dish at 350°F for 20 minutes, if you like.

PER SERVING Calories: 691; Total fat: 34g; Saturated fat: 6g; Cholesterol: 270mg; Carbohydrates: 51g; Fiber: 10g; Protein: 76g

NEXT DAY Use any leftover chicken mixture to make tacos. Heat crisp taco shells according to the package directions. Reheat the chicken mixture in a saucepan on the stove top, and put the mixture in the shells. Top with lettuce, chopped tomatoes, chopped avocado, chopped red onion, and more Cotija cheese.

SPANISH CHICKEN

SERVES 2

PREP
10 MINUTES

COOK
8 HOURS
ON LOW
plus
10 MINUTES
ON HIGH

GLUTEN-FREE

SOY-FREE

NUT-FREE

Also called *arroz con pollo*, this Spanish dish is like a celebration in a pot. It may seem like there are lots of ingredients, but each one plays an important role. You can use chicken thighs or drumsticks, or chicken quarters, which is the thigh and drumstick together.

2 bone-in, skinless chicken quarters

2 teaspoons chili powder

½ teaspoon ground sweet paprika

½ teaspoon salt

⅛ teaspoon ground cayenne pepper

1 onion, chopped

1 green bell pepper, chopped

2 garlic cloves, minced

⅔ cup long-grain brown rice

1 (14-ounce) can diced tomatoes, undrained

1 cup Chicken Stock (page 28)

1 tablespoon freshly squeezed lemon juice

½ teaspoon lemon zest

1 pinch saffron threads

¼ cup sliced green olives

1 cup frozen green peas, thawed

1. On a platter, sprinkle the chicken with the chili powder, paprika, salt, and cayenne pepper. Rub the spices into the chicken.

2. In the slow cooker, combine the onion, bell pepper, garlic, and rice. Top with the chicken quarters.

3. In a medium bowl, mix the tomatoes, stock, lemon juice, lemon zest, and saffron. Let stand 5 minutes, then pour the mixture into the slow cooker. Top with the olives.

4. Cover and cook on low for 7 to 8 hours, or until the chicken registers 165°F on a meat thermometer.

5. Add the peas, cover and cook on high for 10 minutes, and serve.

PER SERVING Calories: 787; Total fat: 32g; Saturated fat: 8g; Cholesterol: 170mg; Carbohydrates: 82g; Fiber: 14g; Protein: 51g

SIX

SEAFOOD

Cooking seafood in the slow cooker can be tricky. Most seafood cooks in just a few minutes, so these recipes have to be designed so the fish or shrimp is added during the last half hour of cooking time. You can use just about any kind of fish in these recipes, as long as you're careful about substitutions. White fish fillets to use include arctic char, red snapper, and grouper. Cod, tuna, and salmon are interchangeable, too.

SHRIMP RISOTTO

SERVES 2

PREP
10 MINUTES

COOK
5½ HOURS
ON LOW
plus
15 MINUTES
ON HIGH

GLUTEN-FREE

SOY-FREE

NUT-FREE

Risotto in the slow cooker cooks to tender perfection, and you don't have to stand at the stove stirring constantly. Paired with shrimp and white wine, this dish will have you thinking about the Mediterranean. You must use Arborio rice, which is a short-grain rice that releases starch as it cooks.

1 onion, chopped

2 garlic cloves, minced

1⅓ cups Arborio rice

½ teaspoon salt

4 cups Chicken Stock (page 28)

¼ cup white wine

¾ pound medium raw shrimp, peeled and deveined

¼ cup grated Parmesan cheese

2 tablespoons butter

1. In the slow cooker, combine the onion, garlic, rice, and salt.

2. Stir in the stock and wine.

3. Cover and cook on low for 5½ hours, or until the rice is tender.

4. Add the shrimp and stir gently; cover and cook on high for 15 minutes, or until the shrimp curl and turn pink.

5. Stir in the cheese and butter, and turn off the slow cooker. Cover and let stand for 10 minutes.

6. Stir again and serve.

PER SERVING Calories: 891; Total fat: 19g; Saturated fat: 11g; Cholesterol: 399mg; Carbohydrates: 115g; Fiber: 5g; Protein: 54g

NEXT DAY Leftover risotto can be turned into delicious risotto cakes. Form cold risotto into patties and coat in bread crumbs. Sauté in melted butter for 4 to 5 minutes per side, turning once, until crisp and golden brown.

PREP
15 MINUTES

COOK
7½ HOURS
ON LOW
plus
30 MINUTES
ON HIGH

GLUTEN-FREE

SOY-FREE

NUT-FREE

SALMON AND WHITE BEANS

SERVES 2

Salmon cooks to tender perfection in the slow cooker, but you must add it during the last half hour of cooking time. Let the side dish of beans and flavor base for the salmon cook while you're at work. Then just add the tomatoes and salmon, set the table, and sit down to a delicious dinner.

1 cup dried navy beans

1 bulb fennel, chopped

3 garlic cloves, minced

3 cups Chicken Stock (page 28)

1 bay leaf

½ teaspoon dried marjoram leaves

¼ teaspoon salt

1 cup chopped grape tomatoes

2 (6-ounce) salmon fillets

½ teaspoon ground paprika

1. Sort the beans and rinse; drain well.

2. In the slow cooker, top the beans with the fennel and garlic. Pour the stock over everything and add the bay leaf, marjoram, and salt.

3. Cover and cook on low for 7½ hours, or until the beans are tender.

4. Remove and discard the bay leaf. Stir in the tomatoes.

5. Sprinkle the salmon with the paprika and place it on top of the beans.

6. Cover and cook on high for 25 to 30 minutes, or until the salmon flakes when tested with a fork, and serve.

PER SERVING Calories: 652; Total fat: 13g; Saturated fat: 2g; Cholesterol: 75mg; Carbohydrates: 78g; Fiber: 30g; Protein: 60g

DID YOU KNOW? Salmon is high in omega-3 fatty acids, which control inflammation in the body and can support heart health. Look for wild-caught Alaskan salmon in the market, such as chum, sockeye, coho, pink, and Chinook, because they have lower levels of contamination and because Alaskan fishing runs are more sustainable.

TUSCAN FISH AND VEGGIES

PREP
20 MINUTES

COOK
7 HOURS
ON LOW
plus
30 MINUTES
ON HIGH

GLUTEN-FREE

SOY-FREE

NUT-FREE

SERVES 2

Tuscany is famous for its wonderful produce, especially bell peppers, eggplant, mushrooms, and potatoes. After the veggies roast all day, you simply add some fish fillets, which poach for a few minutes until tender and moist.

Nonstick cooking spray

1 red bell pepper, cut into strips

1 orange bell pepper, cut into strips

1 onion, chopped

1 small eggplant, peeled and cubed

1 cup sliced mushrooms

2 cups creamer potatoes

3 garlic cloves, minced

1 tablespoon extra-virgin olive oil

1 teaspoon minced fresh rosemary leaves

½ teaspoon dried thyme leaves

½ teaspoon salt

⅛ teaspoon freshly ground black pepper

½ cup Chicken Stock (page 28) or Vegetable Broth (page 27)

2 (6-ounce) grouper or arctic char fillets

1. Spray the slow cooker with the nonstick cooking spray.

2. In the slow cooker, combine the red and orange bell peppers, onion, eggplant, mushrooms, potatoes, and garlic, and drizzle with the olive oil. Sprinkle with the rosemary, thyme, salt, and pepper.

3. Pour the stock over everything.

4. Cover and cook on low for 7 hours, or until the vegetables are tender.

5. Place the fish on top of the vegetables. Cover and cook on high for 20 to 30 minutes, or until the fish flakes when tested with a fork, and serve.

PER SERVING Calories: 499; Total fat: 11g; Saturated fat: 2g; Cholesterol: 80mg; Carbohydrates: 53g; Fiber: 17g; Protein: 50g

SEASONAL SUBSTITUTION In the summer, go to the farmers' market and choose lots of different fresh vegetables for this recipe. You might want to try different varieties of mushrooms, look for purple bell peppers, or add some sliced heirloom tomatoes—and pile on the fresh herbs!

FISH CHOWDER

SERVES 2

PREP
15 MINUTES

COOK
15 MINUTES
ON THE
STOVE TOP
plus
7 HOURS
ON LOW

GLUTEN-FREE

SOY-FREE

NUT-FREE

This fish chowder recipe is rich and thick and full of chunky potatoes and briny seafood. Light cream stirred in at the end keeps the chowder nice and smooth.

3 slices bacon

1 onion, chopped

2 garlic cloves, minced

3 Yukon Gold potatoes, peeled and cubed

1 cup frozen corn

1 cup clam juice

2 cups Chicken Stock (page 28)

½ teaspoon salt

⅛ teaspoon freshly ground black pepper

¼ pound cod, cut into 1-inch pieces

¼ pound bay scallops

¼ pound medium shrimp, peeled and deveined

½ cup light cream

1 tablespoon cornstarch

1 tablespoon minced fresh chives

1. In a small skillet over medium-high heat, cook the bacon until crisp, about 10 minutes. Drain on paper towels, crumble, and set aside in the refrigerator.

2. In the same skillet over medium heat, cook the onion and garlic in the bacon drippings for 5 minutes, or until crisp-tender.

3. In the slow cooker, combine the onion-garlic mixture, potatoes, corn, clam juice, stock, salt, and pepper.

4. Cover and cook on low for 6½ hours, or until the vegetables are tender.

5. Add the cod, cover, and cook on low for 5 minutes.

6. Add the scallops and shrimp.

7. In a small bowl, mix the cream and cornstarch well. Stir the mixture into the slow cooker. Cover and cook on low for 10 minutes, or until the shrimp curl and turn pink and all the seafood is cooked.

8. Garnish with the bacon crumbles and chives and serve.

PER SERVING Calories: 770; Total fat: 25g; Saturated fat: 10g; Cholesterol: 226mg; Carbohydrates: 87g; Fiber: 7g; Protein: 55g

PREP
20 MINUTES

COOK
7 HOURS
ON LOW
plus
30 MINUTES
ON HIGH

GLUTEN-FREE

SOY-FREE

NUT-FREE

ITALIAN SEAFOOD STEW

SERVES 2

This stew is rich with lots of vegetables, fish, and shellfish. You can substitute your favorite vegetables; just make sure to fill the slow cooker about two-thirds full before you add the fish. Garnish with plenty of fresh herbs and a drizzle of extra-virgin olive oil.

1 onion, chopped

1 fennel bulb, chopped

2 carrots, sliced

1 celery stalk, sliced

1 large tomato, seeded and chopped

2 cups small red potatoes

1½ cups Chicken Stock (page 28) or Vegetable Broth (page 27)

¼ cup dry white wine

½ teaspoon dried thyme leaves

½ teaspoon dried marjoram leaves

½ teaspoon salt

⅛ teaspoon freshly ground black pepper

1 cod fillet, cut into 1-inch pieces

1 cup medium raw shrimp, peeled and deveined

8 clams, scrubbed

1. In the slow cooker, combine the onion, fennel, carrots, celery, tomato, and potatoes. Pour the stock and wine over everything. Add the thyme, marjoram, salt, and pepper, and stir well.

2. Cover and cook on low for 7 hours, or until the vegetables are tender.

3. Add the cod, cover, and cook on high for 10 minutes.

4. Add the shrimp and clams, cover, and cook on high for 15 to 20 minutes more, or until the shrimp curl and turn pink and the clams open, and serve.

PER SERVING Calories: 488; Total fat: 4g; Saturated fat: 0g; Cholesterol: 93mg; Carbohydrates: 66g; Fiber: 11g; Protein: 42g

PREP IT RIGHT When cooking shellfish such as mussels or clams, there are a few rules to follow. Only cook shellfish that are tightly closed. If any do not close when they are tapped, discard them. After cooking, only eat shellfish that are open. Discard any that do not open during cooking.

SALMON CREOLE

SERVES 2

PREP
15 MINUTES

COOK
7½ HOURS
ON LOW
plus
20 MINUTES
ON HIGH

GLUTEN-FREE

SOY-FREE

NUT-FREE

Creole stew, which is usually made with shrimp or chicken, is made with lots of tomatoes and vegetables, including onions and garlic. The vegetable mixture cooks for hours, and then cubed salmon is stirred in toward the end of cooking time. This is an ultra-healthy stew, with loads of veggies and omega-3-rich salmon, that you're likely to find yourself making again and again. Serve with crusty bread to sop up the juices.

1 (14-ounce) can diced tomatoes, undrained

3 tablespoons tomato paste

1 onion, chopped

1 cup sliced cremini mushrooms

3 celery stalks and their leaves, sliced

1 green bell pepper, chopped

3 garlic cloves, minced

1 cup Chicken Stock (page 28)

1 teaspoon ground sweet paprika

½ teaspoon dried oregano leaves

½ teaspoon dried basil leaves

¼ teaspoon dried thyme leaves

½ teaspoon salt

¼ teaspoon freshly ground black pepper

¼ teaspoon crushed red pepper flakes

2 (6-ounce) salmon fillets, cubed

1. In the slow cooker, combine all the ingredients except the salmon.

2. Cover and cook on low for 7½ hours, or until the vegetables are tender.

3. Add the salmon to the slow cooker and stir.

4. Cover and cook on high for 15 to 20 minutes, or until the salmon flakes when tested with a fork, and serve.

PER SERVING Calories: 360; Total fat: 12g; Saturated fat: 2g; Cholesterol: 75mg; Carbohydrates: 28g; Fiber: 8g; Protein: 39g

DID YOU KNOW? The combination of onions, celery, and bell peppers is known as the "holy trinity" in southern cooking. These vegetables start many of the South's most famous dishes, including jambalaya, gumbo, and étouffée.

PREP
20 MINUTES

COOK
6½ HOURS
ON LOW
plus
30 MINUTES
ON HIGH

GLUTEN-FREE

SOY-FREE

NUT-FREE

MUSSELS WITH TOMATO CURRY

SERVES 2

This tangy tomato curry is just delicious with tender, briny mussels. Be sure to scrub the mussels and pull off the beards (tiny threads the shellfish use to attach themselves to rocks) before you cook them.

2 (14-ounce) cans diced tomatoes, undrained

½ cup dry white wine or clam juice

1 bunch green onions, cut into 1-inch pieces

2 shallots, minced

3 garlic cloves, minced

2 teaspoons Curry Rub (page 23)

2 pounds mussels, scrubbed

1. In the slow cooker, combine all the ingredients except the mussels.

2. Cover and cook on low for 6½ hours.

3. Add the mussels, cover, and cook on high for 30 minutes, or until the mussels open, and serve.

PER SERVING Calories: 547; Total fat: 11g; Saturated fat: 2g; Cholesterol: 127mg; Carbohydrates: 42g; Fiber: 7g; Protein: 59g

JAMBALAYA

SERVES 2

PREP
20 MINUTES

COOK
7½ HOURS
ON LOW
plus
20 MINUTES
ON HIGH

GLUTEN-FREE

SOY-FREE

NUT-FREE

A classic, spicy Cajun dish with loads of seafood, vegetables, and heady aromatics, jambalaya is always a treat for the senses. Try adding some fully cooked sausage along with the vegetables to this recipe, if you like.

1 onion, chopped

1 green bell pepper, chopped

2 celery stalks, sliced

4 garlic cloves, minced

1 (14-ounce) can diced tomatoes, undrained

2 tablespoons tomato paste

1 teaspoon jerk rub

½ teaspoon dried thyme leaves

½ teaspoon dried oregano leaves

½ teaspoon salt

¼ teaspoon freshly ground black pepper

⅛ teaspoon crushed red pepper flakes

1 cup clam juice

¾ cup Chicken Stock (page 28)

½ pound raw shrimp, peeled and deveined

2 grouper fillets, cut into 1-inch pieces

1. In the slow cooker, combine all the ingredients except the shrimp and grouper.

2. Cover and cook on low for 7½ hours.

3. Add the shrimp and grouper fillets, cover, and cook on high for 15 to 20 minutes, or until the shrimp curl and turn pink and the fish is firm, and serve.

PER SERVING Calories: 568; Total fat: 6g; Saturated fat: 2g; Cholesterol: 345mg; Carbohydrates: 38g; Fiber: 7g; Protein: 87g

SEVEN

MEATLESS MEALS

Slow-cooked vegetarian food has a reputation for being bland and boring. Not true with these recipes! Season the food generously with fresh herbs, which are readily available at all supermarkets these days, and be sure to taste and add more seasoning if needed before you eat.

BLACK BEANS AND POLENTA

SERVES 2

In this recipe, two slow cooker cooking bags—one to cook creamy polenta, the other to cook the colorful black beans and veggies—act like two slow cookers! Spoon the lush polenta onto your plate, and top with the black bean mixture.

2½ cups Vegetable Broth (page 27) or water

1 tablespoon butter

½ teaspoon salt, divided

⅔ cup yellow cornmeal or polenta

⅓ cup frozen corn, thawed

1 (14-ounce) can black beans, rinsed and drained

1 onion, chopped

1 red bell pepper, chopped

2 garlic cloves, minced

1 tomato, seeded and chopped

2 teaspoons chili powder

½ teaspoon dried oregano leaves

⅛ teaspoon freshly ground black pepper

1. In a small saucepan over high heat, combine the broth, butter, and ¼ teaspoon of salt, and bring just to steaming. Stir in the cornmeal and corn.

2. Pour the mixture into a slow cooker cooking bag and place it in the slow cooker, taking up half the area.

3. In another slow cooker bag, combine the black beans, onion, bell pepper, garlic, tomato, chili powder, oregano, the remaining ¼ teaspoon of salt, and the pepper. Place in the slow cooker.

4. Make sure the bag tops are over the side of the slow cooker.

5. Cover and cook on low for 6 hours, or until the polenta is tender, and serve.

PER SERVING Calories: 580; Total fat: 10g; Saturated fat: 4g; Cholesterol: 15mg; Carbohydrates: 104g; Fiber: 27g; Protein: 24g

DID YOU KNOW? Black beans and corn are excellent complementary sources of protein, making them an ideal nutritional combination for vegans and vegetarians.

PREP
20 MINUTES

COOK
6 MINUTES
ON THE
STOVE TOP
plus
7 HOURS
ON LOW

SOY-FREE

NUT-FREE

VEGETARIAN

VEGETABLE LASAGNA

SERVES 2

Yes, you can make lasagna in the slow cooker, as long as you follow a couple of rules. First, use no-boil noodles. Those are noodles that are precooked, so they soften easily without a lot of liquid. And second, layer ingredients evenly so everything cooks at the same time. Follow these simple rules and you'll have a cheesy, toothsome lasagna.

1 tablespoon extra-virgin olive oil

1 onion, chopped

2 garlic cloves, minced

2½ cups Marinara Sauce (page 36), divided

1½ cups ricotta cheese

⅓ cup grated Parmesan cheese

Nonstick cooking spray

6 to 8 no-boil lasagna noodles, divided

1 cup chopped baby spinach leaves, divided

⅔ cup shredded mozzarella cheese

½ teaspoon ground paprika

1. In a small saucepan over medium heat, heat the olive oil. Sauté the onion and garlic until tender, about 6 minutes. Remove from the heat and stir in the marinara sauce.

2. In a small bowl, mix the ricotta cheese with the Parmesan.

3. Line the slow cooker with heavy-duty foil and spray with nonstick cooking spray.

4. Put one-third of the marinara mixture in the slow cooker. Top with half of the noodles, breaking some to fit if necessary.

5. Top the noodles with half of the cheese mixture, followed by half of the spinach.

6. Add half of the remaining marinara mixture and the remaining noodles, cheese mixture, and spinach. Top with the remaining marinara mixture.

7. Sprinkle with the mozzarella cheese and paprika.

8. Cover and cook on low for 7 hours, or until the noodles are tender when pierced with a fork.

9. Turn off the slow cooker and let stand, covered, for 30 minutes.

10. Using the foil, lift the lasagna out of the slow cooker. Slice and serve.

PER SERVING Calories: 1050; Total fat: 43g; Saturated fat: 20g; Cholesterol: 129mg; Carbohydrates: 111g; Fiber: 10g; Protein: 56g

RICE-STUFFED PEPPERS

SERVES 2

PREP
20 MINUTES

COOK
5 MINUTES
ON THE
STOVE TOP
plus
6½ HOURS
ON LOW
and
30 MINUTES
ON HIGH

GLUTEN-FREE

SOY-FREE

VEGAN

Most stuffed pepper recipes require you to precook the peppers so they are nice and tender by the time the filling is done. Well, when you use the slow cooker, you can skip this step. This easy recipe with nutty long-grain rice and pine nuts melding with tomato-y aromatics is delicious for dinner on a weeknight.

3 large bell peppers

1 tablespoon extra-virgin olive oil

1 onion, chopped

2 garlic cloves, minced

½ cup chopped, seeded tomato

⅓ cup long-grain rice

2 tablespoons pine nuts

½ teaspoon salt

½ teaspoon dried oregano

⅛ teaspoon freshly ground black pepper

¾ cup Vegetable Broth (page 27), divided

Nonstick cooking spray

1. Cut the tops off the bell peppers. Remove and discard the membranes and seeds, and set the peppers aside.

2. In a medium saucepan over medium heat, heat the oil. Add the onion and garlic and cook, stirring, until tender, about 5 minutes.

3. Remove the pan from the heat and stir in the tomato, rice, pine nuts, salt, oregano, black pepper, and ½ cup of broth. Stuff the peppers with this mixture, being sure to include the liquid.

4. Spray the slow cooker with the nonstick cooking spray. Add the peppers and pour the remaining ¼ cup of broth around them.

5. Cover and cook on low for 6½ hours.

continued

6. Spoon some of the liquid in the bottom of the slow cooker into the peppers.

7. Cover and cook on high for 30 minutes, until the rice is tender, and serve.

PER SERVING Calories: 371; Total fat: 15g; Saturated fat: 2g; Cholesterol: 0mg; Carbohydrates: 52g; Fiber: 8g; Protein: 9g

NEXT DAY If you have a leftover stuffed pepper, refrigerate it. The next day, remove the filling and chop the pepper; mix the chopped pepper with the rest of the filling. Use this mixture to fill an omelet; add some shredded cheese, and enjoy.

HOPPIN' JOHN

SERVES 2

PREP
15 MINUTES

COOK
7 HOURS
ON LOW
plus
30 MINUTES
ON HIGH

GLUTEN-FREE

SOY-FREE

NUT-FREE

VEGAN

Hoppin' John is usually made with bacon or a ham hock, but here, this simple southern black-eyed pea stew with rice and collard greens gets a rich, meaty flavor from porcini mushrooms and their soaking liquid. Typically eaten on New Year's Eve for luck in the New Year, it's delicious any season.

1 ounce dried porcini mushrooms

½ cup warm water

⅔ cup dried black-eyed peas, sorted and rinsed

1 onion, chopped

1 red bell pepper, chopped

4 garlic cloves, minced

½ cup brown long-grain rice

2½ cups Vegetable Broth (page 27)

1 bay leaf

½ teaspoon dried marjoram leaves

½ teaspoon salt

¼ teaspoon freshly ground black pepper

⅛ teaspoon crushed red pepper flakes

1 large tomato, seeded and chopped

2 cups chopped collard greens

1. In a small bowl, combine the mushrooms and warm water. Let stand for 20 minutes. Strain the mushrooms, reserving the soaking liquid. Chop the mushrooms and strain the soaking liquid through cheesecloth.

2. In the slow cooker, combine all the ingredients, including the strained soaking liquid, except the tomato and collard greens.

3. Cover and cook on low for 7 hours. Remove and discard the bay leaf.

continued

4. Add the tomato and collard greens to the slow cooker and stir.

5. Cover and cook on high for 30 minutes, or until the greens are tender, and serve.

PER SERVING Calories: 399; Total fat: 4g; Saturated fat: 1g; Cholesterol: 0mg; Carbohydrates: 71g; Fiber: 14g; Protein: 21g

SPANISH RICE WITH BLACK BEANS

SERVES 2

PREP
15 MINUTES

COOK
6 MINUTES
ON THE
STOVE TOP
plus
7 HOURS
ON LOW

GLUTEN-FREE

SOY-FREE

NUT-FREE

VEGAN

Spanish rice is also known as dirty rice, or rice with a lot of ingredients that range from ground beef to bell peppers and onion. This vegan version—studded with bell pepper, black beans, and tomato, all seasoned to perfection with aromatic garlic, onion, chili powder, and oregano—is delicious.

1 tablespoon extra-virgin olive oil

1 onion, chopped

3 garlic cloves, minced

⅔ cup long-grain brown rice

1 green bell pepper, chopped

1 (14-ounce) can black beans, rinsed and drained

1 (14-ounce) can diced tomatoes, undrained

⅔ cup Vegetable Broth (page 27)

2 teaspoons chili powder

½ teaspoon dried oregano

1. In a small saucepan over medium heat, heat the olive oil. Add the onion and garlic and sauté, stirring occasionally, until crisp-tender, about 5 minutes.

2. Stir in the rice and cook, stirring constantly, for 1 minute.

3. In the slow cooker, combine the rice mixture with all the remaining ingredients, and stir.

4. Cover and cook on low for 6 to 7 hours, or until the rice is tender.

PER SERVING Calories: 654; Total fat: 11g; Saturated fat: 2g; Cholesterol: 0mg; Carbohydrates: 116g; Fiber: 26g; Protein: 28g

PREP
20 MINUTES

COOK
7 HOURS
ON LOW

GLUTEN-FREE

SOY-FREE

NUT-FREE

VEGETARIAN

QUINOA-STUFFED ONIONS

SERVES 2

Stuffed onions are like stuffed peppers, with a bit more bite to them. Here, they're filled with bright bell pepper, tangy kale, spicy salsa, and nutty quinoa, an ancient grain that is a complete source of protein.

3 large yellow onions, peeled

2 garlic cloves, minced

1 red bell pepper, chopped

½ cup chopped kale

½ cup uncooked quinoa, well rinsed

1¼ cups Red Salsa (page 41)

½ teaspoon dried thyme leaves

½ teaspoon salt

⅛ teaspoon freshly ground black pepper

6 tablespoons Vegetable Broth (page 27)

¼ cup water

⅔ cup shredded Cheddar cheese

1. Cut a small slice off the bottom (root end) of each onion so it will sit upright.

2. Carefully remove the centers of the onions, making sure to leave a ½-inch shell so the onions will stay together while cooking. Reserve the centers for another recipe.

3. In a medium bowl, mix the garlic, bell pepper, kale, quinoa, salsa, thyme, salt, and pepper. Spoon the mixture into the onions.

4. Pour the broth over the filling in the onions. Place the onions in the slow cooker and pour the water around the onions.

5. Cover and cook on low for 7 hours, or until the onions are tender and the quinoa is cooked.

6. Top with the cheese; let stand, covered, for 5 minutes; and serve.

PER SERVING Calories: 501; Total fat: 18g; Saturated fat: 9g; Cholesterol: 45mg; Carbohydrates: 66g; Fiber: 12g; Protein: 24g

PREP IT RIGHT Always rinse quinoa well before cooking to remove the bitter coating called saponin. Some quinoa is prerinsed, but it doesn't hurt to rinse it again.

THAI VEGGIES AND BEANS

SERVES 2

PREP
20 MINUTES

COOK
7½ HOURS
ON LOW
plus
30 MINUTES
ON HIGH

GLUTEN-FREE
————
NUT-FREE
————
VEGAN
————

The heating (hot chiles, ginger) and cooling (lemongrass, Thai basil) ingredients in this stew meld together into a delicious mélange. Together with eggplant, mushrooms, and beans, this one-pot meal becomes a complete protein. Who says you need meat for that?

1 onion, chopped

4 garlic cloves, minced

1 small eggplant, peeled and cubed

1 cup sliced shiitake mushrooms

1 small red chile pepper, minced

1 stalk lemongrass, bent in half

2 teaspoons grated fresh ginger

1 (14-ounce) can cannellini beans, rinsed and drained

⅓ cup Vegetable Broth (page 27)

1 tablespoon low-sodium soy sauce

1 cup green beans

1 cup thinly sliced bok choy

1 tablespoon minced fresh Thai basil or regular basil

1. In the slow cooker, combine the onion, garlic, eggplant, mushrooms, chile pepper, lemongrass, ginger, and cannellini beans.

2. Pour the broth and soy sauce over everything.

3. Cover and cook on low for 7½ hours, or until the vegetables are tender. Remove and discard the lemongrass.

4. Add the green beans and bok choy. Cover and cook on high for 30 minutes.

5. Stir well, garnish with the Thai basil, and serve.

PER SERVING Calories: 333; Total fat: 3g; Saturated fat: 0g; Cholesterol: 0mg; Carbohydrates: 68g; Fiber: 22g; Protein: 16g

PREP
15 MINUTES

COOK
8 HOURS
ON LOW

GLUTEN-FREE

SOY-FREE

NUT-FREE

VEGAN

INDIAN LENTILS

SERVES 2

Lentils are edible pulses, which are the seeds of a plant in the legume family. They are high in protein and fiber and low in fat and don't need to be soaked before cooking. Lentils are delicious cooked with Indian spices in this colorful, sunny dish, also known as dal.

⅛ teaspoon saffron threads

¼ cup warm water

⅔ cup dried red lentils, sorted and rinsed

⅓ cup dried yellow split peas, sorted and rinsed

1 onion, chopped

1 red bell pepper, chopped

3 garlic cloves, minced

2 large tomatoes, seeded and chopped

2 teaspoons grated fresh ginger

1 teaspoon Curry Rub (page 23)

1 teaspoon yellow curry paste

2 cups Vegetable Broth (page 27)

½ teaspoon salt

⅛ teaspoon freshly ground black pepper

½ cup coconut milk

1. In a small bowl, soak the saffron threads in the water for 10 minutes.

2. In the slow cooker, combine the lentils, peas, onion, bell pepper, garlic, tomatoes, ginger, curry rub, curry paste, broth, salt, and pepper.

3. Stir in the saffron and soaking liquid.

4. Cover and cook on low for 8 hours, or until the lentils and peas are very tender.

5. Stir in the coconut milk and serve.

PER SERVING Calories: 661; Total fat: 19g; Saturated fat: 13g; Cholesterol: 0mg; Carbohydrates: 89g; Fiber: 39g; Protein: 37g

PERFECT PAIR Serve this warm and rich, thick stew with a fresh tomato salad. Combine 2 large tomatoes, seeded and chopped, with ¼ cup chopped sweet onion, 2 tablespoons torn cilantro leaves, ¼ teaspoon salt, and a sprinkle of pepper. Drizzle with 1 tablespoon extra-virgin olive oil and 1 tablespoon lemon juice, and serve.

GLUTEN-FREE

SOY-FREE

NUT-FREE

VEGETARIAN

CORN AND BEAN ENCHILADA BAKE

SERVES 2

Sweet corn and savory beans make for a delicious combination in these enchiladas. The spicy cheese, salsa, and jalapeño pepper are the perfect complement to this festive meal.

1 onion, chopped

3 garlic cloves, minced

1 jalapeño pepper, minced

1 (14-ounce) can black beans, rinsed and drained

1 cup frozen corn, thawed

1 large tomato, seeded and chopped

Nonstick cooking spray

1¼ cups Salsa Verde (page 39), divided

6 corn tortillas

⅔ cup shredded pepper Jack cheese, divided

1. In a medium bowl, mix the onion, garlic, jalapeño pepper, beans, corn, and tomato.

2. Spray the slow cooker with the nonstick cooking spray.

3. Put ⅓ cup of the salsa verde in the bottom of the slow cooker.

4. Top with 3 of the tortillas, half of the bean mixture, half of the remaining salsa, and half of the cheese.

5. Repeat the layers, ending with the cheese.

6. Cover and cook on low for 6 hours, or until the tortillas are soft and the mixture is bubbling, and serve.

PER SERVING Calories: 679; Total fat: 14g; Saturated fat: 7g; Cholesterol: 25mg; Carbohydrates: 112g; Fiber: 27g; Protein: 35g

CURRIED VEGGIE BAKE

SERVES 2

With its abundance of colorful veggies, toothsome tofu, and a hint of pepperiness, this casserole is simply wonderful piled over steaming brown rice or whole-wheat pasta. While the list of ingredients may appear long, this recipe is still super easy since there's no stove prep, and all the ingredients go into the slow cooker at once.

1 (8-ounce) block extra-firm tofu

1 small eggplant, peeled and cubed

1 onion, chopped

2 garlic cloves, minced

1 red bell pepper, sliced

1 cup sliced mushrooms

2 teaspoons curry powder

1 teaspoon red curry paste

½ cup Vegetable Broth (page 27)

½ cup almond milk

½ teaspoon dried marjoram leaves

½ teaspoon dried thyme leaves

¼ teaspoon salt

⅛ teaspoon freshly ground black pepper

1. Press the tofu between paper towels, using your hands and pressing hard, until dry. Cut the tofu into cubes.

2. In the slow cooker, combine all the ingredients and stir.

3. Cover and cook on low for 6 to 7 hours, or until the vegetables are tender, and serve.

PER SERVING Calories: 382; Total fat: 22g; Saturated fat: 14g; Cholesterol: 0mg; Carbohydrates: 34g; Fiber: 14g; Protein: 20g

PREP
15 MINUTES
plus
OVERNIGHT
TO SOAK

COOK
8 HOURS
ON LOW

GLUTEN-FREE

SOY-FREE

NUT-FREE

VEGAN

RED BEANS AND RICE

SERVES 2

This classic southern dish is usually made with sausage and/or ham hocks, but it's also delicious without meat. Add more jalapeño peppers or serrano peppers if you like your food extra spicy. The beans soak overnight before cooking, so plan ahead.

1 cup dried red kidney beans

1 onion, chopped

1 green bell pepper, chopped

2 celery stalks, chopped

3 garlic cloves, minced

1 jalapeño pepper, minced

1 bay leaf

½ teaspoon dried oregano

½ teaspoon salt

¼ teaspoon Tabasco sauce

⅛ teaspoon freshly ground black pepper

3 cups Vegetable Broth (page 27)

2 cups hot cooked rice

1. In a medium bowl, cover the beans with cool water. Cover the bowl with foil and let stand overnight.

2. In the morning, drain the beans, discarding the soaking water. Rinse well.

3. In the slow cooker, combine the beans, onion, bell pepper, celery, garlic, jalapeño pepper, bay leaf, oregano, salt, Tabasco sauce, and pepper, and stir.

4. Pour the broth into the slow cooker.

5. Cover and cook on low for 8 hours, or until the beans are tender. Remove and discard the bay leaf.

6. Serve over the hot cooked rice.

PER SERVING Calories: 740; Total fat: 4g; Saturated fat: 1g; Cholesterol: 0mg; Carbohydrates: 140g; Fiber: 18g; Protein: 35g

PREP IT RIGHT Soak kidney beans overnight for even cooking and to help remove a toxic, tongue-twisting compound called phytohaemagglutinin. Cooking in the slow cooker eliminates it completely.

VEGETABLE POT PIE

SERVES 2

PREP
20 MINUTES

COOK
5 MINUTES
ON THE
STOVE TOP
plus
7 HOURS
ON LOW

SOY-FREE

NUT-FREE

VEGETARIAN

This robust vegetarian pot pie, with a hint of spiciness, gives the veggies and beans their due with long, simmered cooking. Though the traditional pot pie is topped with a pie crust, that's one thing the slow cooker can't do. This recipe uses a slightly sweet cornbread mixture instead.

Nonstick cooking spray

1 tablespoon extra-virgin olive oil

1 onion, chopped

2 garlic cloves, minced

1 jalapeño pepper, minced

2 carrots, sliced

1 (15-ounce) can chickpeas, rinsed and drained

1 cup frozen corn, thawed

½ cup Vegetable Broth (page 27)

½ cup plus 2 tablespoons all-purpose flour, divided

1 teaspoon chili powder

¾ teaspoon salt, divided

½ teaspoon dried marjoram leaves

⅛ teaspoon freshly ground black pepper

1 cup yellow cornmeal

½ teaspoon baking powder

⅔ cup buttermilk

1 egg

2 tablespoons butter, melted

½ teaspoon ground smoked paprika

1. Spray the slow cooker with the nonstick cooking spray.

2. In a small saucepan over medium heat, heat the olive oil. Add the onion, garlic, jalapeño pepper, and carrots; sauté, stirring, until crisp-tender, about 5 minutes.

3. In the slow cooker, combine the onion mixture with the chickpeas and corn.

4. In a small bowl, stir together the broth and 2 tablespoons of flour. Stir the mixture into the slow cooker.

continued

5. Add the chili powder, ½ teaspoon of salt, marjoram, and pepper, and stir.

6. In a medium bowl, mix the cornmeal, the remaining ½ cup of flour, baking powder, and the remaining ¼ teaspoon of salt. Stir in the buttermilk, egg, and melted butter.

7. Pour the cornmeal mixture into the slow cooker. Sprinkle with the paprika.

8. Cover and cook on low for 6 to 7 hours, or until a toothpick inserted in the center of the cornbread topping comes out clean, and serve.

PER SERVING Calories: 981; Total fat: 32g; Saturated fat: 11g; Cholesterol: 116mg; Carbohydrates: 144g; Fiber: 19g; Protein: 35g

MEXICAN LASAGNA

SERVES 2

Refried beans and veggies replace tomato sauce and meat in this Mexican vegetarian version of the classic lasagna. Instead of pasta, we'll use corn tortillas, which soften as they cook, in this hearty layered dish. You can line the appliance with foil so you can lift out the whole thing, or just scoop out portions when it's done.

1 (14-ounce) can diced tomatoes, undrained

1 cup canned refried beans

2 teaspoons chili powder

½ teaspoon salt

⅛ teaspoon freshly ground black pepper

1 onion, chopped

3 garlic cloves, minced

1 jalapeño pepper, minced

⅓ cup sliced black olives

1 cup frozen corn, thawed

1 cup Red Salsa (page 41), divided

Nonstick cooking spray (optional)

5 or 6 corn tortillas

1 cup shredded pepper Jack cheese, divided

1. In a medium bowl, mix the tomatoes and beans well. Add the chili powder, salt, and pepper.

2. In another medium bowl, mix the onion, garlic, jalapeño pepper, olives, corn, and ½ cup of salsa.

3. Spray the slow cooker with nonstick cooking spray, or line it with heavy-duty foil.

4. Place ¼ cup of the salsa on the bottom of the slow cooker. Add enough tortillas to cover, tearing to fit as necessary.

continued

5. Top the tortillas with half of the refried bean mixture and half of the onion mixture. Top that with half of the cheese.

6. Top the cheese with the remaining tortillas, tearing to fit. Add the remaining bean mixture, onion mixture, and ¼ cup of salsa. Top with the remaining cheese.

7. Cover and cook on low for 7 hours, or until the mixture is hot and bubbly, and serve.

PER SERVING Calories: 644; Total fat: 22g; Saturated fat: 11g; Cholesterol: 55mg; Carbohydrates: 93g; Fiber: 21g; Protein: 29g

PERFECT PAIR This recipe should be served with lots of condiments. Offer more shredded cheese, chopped fresh tomatoes, avocados or guacamole, sour cream, and olives, and let diners garnish their own.

SPICY BLACK-EYED PEAS WITH CORN

PREP
10 MINUTES

COOK
8 HOURS
ON LOW

GLUTEN-FREE

SOY-FREE

NUT-FREE

VEGAN

SERVES 2

Black-eyed peas are creamy white in color, with a small black dot on the pea's (or bean's) curve. They have a wonderful creamy texture and do not get mushy, even when cooked for a long time. This recipe is delicious, with lots of veggies and spices.

1 cup dried black-eyed peas, sorted and rinsed

1 onion, chopped

1 red bell pepper, chopped

2 garlic cloves, minced

1 small zucchini, peeled and chopped

1 cup frozen corn

2 cups Vegetable Broth (page 27)

1 chipotle pepper in adobo sauce, minced

2 teaspoons chili powder

½ teaspoon dried oregano leaves

½ teaspoon salt

⅛ teaspoon freshly ground black pepper

⅛ teaspoon ground cayenne pepper

1. In the slow cooker, combine all the ingredients and stir.

2. Cover and cook on low for 8 hours, or until the beans and vegetables are tender.

3. Stir and serve over hot cooked rice, if desired.

PER SERVING Calories: 357; Total fat: 3g; Saturated fat: 1g; Cholesterol: 0mg; Carbohydrates: 78g; Fiber: 28g; Protein: 27g

BRAZILIAN BLACK BEAN STEW

PREP
20 MINUTES

COOK
8 HOURS
ON LOW

NUT-FREE

VEGAN

SERVES 2

Brazilian recipes are usually made with several different types of meat. To get a hint of that meaty flavor, we'll add tomato paste and soy sauce to this spicy stew. A garnish of chopped fresh cilantro and a drizzle of lime juice give the dish a dash of brightness.

2 cups Vegetable Broth (page 27)

2 tablespoons tomato paste

1 tablespoon soy sauce

2 teaspoons chili powder

½ teaspoon ground cumin

½ teaspoon salt

1 onion, chopped

4 garlic cloves, minced

1 serrano pepper, minced

1 chipotle pepper in adobo sauce, minced

1 large sweet potato, peeled and cubed

1 (15-ounce) can black beans, rinsed and drained

1 large tomato, seeded and chopped

½ cup frozen corn, thawed

1 tablespoon freshly squeezed lime juice

¼ cup chopped fresh cilantro

1 avocado, peeled and cubed

1. In the slow cooker, combine the broth, tomato paste, soy sauce, chili powder, cumin, and salt, and stir to dissolve the tomato paste.

2. Add the onion, garlic, serrano pepper, chipotle pepper, sweet potato, black beans, tomato, corn, and lime juice to the slow cooker, and stir.

3. Cover and cook on low for 7 to 8 hours, or until the sweet potatoes are tender.

4. Garnish with the cilantro and avocado, and serve.

PER SERVING Calories: 731; Total fat: 24g; Saturated fat: 5g; Cholesterol: 0mg; Carbohydrates: 107g; Fiber: 36g; Protein: 32g

DID YOU KNOW? Chipotle peppers are jalapeño peppers that have been smoked. They are usually sold packed in adobo sauce, a tangy red sauce with a smoky flavor. You can use both the chiles and the sauce in recipes. If a recipe calls for just the peppers (like this one does), remove one, but leave some of the sauce on it.

PREP
15 MINUTES

COOK
8 HOURS
ON LOW

GLUTEN-FREE

SOY-FREE

NUT-FREE

VEGETARIAN

BARLEY–BLACK BEAN BURRITOS

SERVES 2

Barley is an ideal grain for the slow cooker. Make sure to purchase pearled barley, not hulled or instant, for this recipe. Combined with black beans, cheese, lots of veggies, and corn tortillas, this hearty recipe is a meal in one.

½ cup pearl barley

Nonstick cooking spray

1 (15-ounce) can black beans, rinsed and drained

1 onion, chopped

3 garlic cloves, minced

1 chipotle pepper in adobo sauce, minced

1 jalapeño pepper

1 cup frozen corn

1 cup Vegetable Broth (page 27)

2 teaspoons chili powder

½ teaspoon ground paprika

½ teaspoon ground cumin

½ teaspoon salt

⅛ teaspoon ground cayenne pepper

6 corn tortillas

1 cup shredded pepper Jack cheese

½ cup Salsa Verde (page 39)

1. Rinse the barley, and drain. Spray the slow cooker with nonstick cooking spray.

2. Combine the barley, beans, onion, garlic, chipotle and jalapeño peppers, corn, broth, chili powder, paprika, cumin, salt, and cayenne pepper in the slow cooker, and stir.

3. Cover and cook on low for 8 hours, until the barley is tender.

4. Make the burritos with the corn tortillas, cheese, barley mixture, and Salsa Verde, and serve.

PER SERVING Calories: 877; Total fat: 15g; Saturated fat: 7g; Cholesterol: 30mg; Carbohydrates: 151g; Fiber: 38g; Protein: 42g

DID YOU KNOW? Burritos are eaten by hand in Mexico. Any type of filling is just rolled up in corn or flour tortillas. Then dig in. You can also fry burritos (called chimichangas). Roll up the burrito, tucking in the ends, and deep fry in 375°F oil until brown, about 5 minutes, and serve.

VEGETARIAN GUMBO

PREP
20 MINUTES

COOK
6 MINUTES
ON THE
STOVE TOP
plus
8 HOURS
ON LOW

SERVES 2

Gumbo is a Creole dish that originated in southern Louisiana. It usually includes meat and shellfish, but this vegetarian version is just as richly flavored as the original. It always includes the "holy trinity" of southern vegetables: onions, celery, and bell peppers.

1 tablespoon extra-virgin olive oil

1 onion, chopped

2 garlic cloves, minced

1 green bell pepper, chopped

1 celery stalk, sliced

1 large tomato, seeded and chopped

1 cup sliced cremini mushrooms

½ cup chopped kale

½ cup sliced okra

½ cup long-grain brown rice

2 cups Vegetable Broth (page 27)

1 bay leaf

½ teaspoon dried thyme leaves

½ teaspoon ground smoked paprika

½ teaspoon salt

⅛ teaspoon Tabasco sauce

⅛ teaspoon ground cayenne pepper

1 tablespoon freshly squeezed lemon juice

1. In a small saucepan over medium heat, heat the olive oil; add the onion and garlic and cook until tender, about 6 minutes, stirring frequently.

2. In the slow cooker, combine the onion and garlic with all the remaining ingredients except the lemon juice, and stir.

3. Cover and cook on low for 8 hours.

4. Remove and discard the bay leaf, stir in the lemon juice, and serve.

PER SERVING Calories: 341; Total fat: 10g; Saturated fat: 2g; Cholesterol: 0mg; Carbohydrates: 53g; Fiber: 7g; Protein: 12g

EIGHT

BEANS & GRAINS

In the slow cooker, beans become very creamy and cook evenly. Make sure you always sort and rinse dried beans before you cook them. Grains are a little trickier to cook in the slow cooker. The best rice to use in the slow cooker is brown rice, since it takes longer to cook. Grains such as farro and barley work well, too.

HERBED POLENTA

PREP
5 MINUTES

COOK
5 MINUTES
ON THE
STOVE TOP
plus
7 HOURS
ON LOW

MAKES 7 CUPS

GLUTEN-FREE

SOY-FREE

NUT-FREE

VEGETARIAN

Polenta is the Italian name for cornmeal porridge, also known as "grits." It is rich and creamy and can be served with stews, casseroles, and grilled meats as a substitute for potatoes. You can make it from plain old cornmeal, or buy polenta or grits—just don't buy instant polenta for this recipe.

5 cups Vegetable Broth (page 27)

2 onions, chopped

4 garlic cloves, minced

1½ teaspoons salt

¼ cup butter

1½ cups cornmeal

¼ cup chopped fresh flat-leaf parsley

3 tablespoons minced fresh basil

2 tablespoons minced fresh thyme

1 cup grated Parmesan cheese

1. In a large saucepan over high heat, bring the broth, onions, garlic, salt, and butter to a boil. Turn down the heat and simmer for 5 minutes, or until the onions are crisp-tender.

2. Carefully pour the hot broth mixture into the slow cooker. Add the cornmeal, stirring constantly with a wire whisk until well combined.

3. Cover and cook on low for 7 hours.

4. Stir in the basil, thyme, and cheese, and serve immediately. Or pour the mixture into a large glass casserole dish and chill overnight. Slice into 4-inch squares, and freeze for up to 4 months.

PER SERVING (1 cup) Calories: 251; Total fat: 12g; Saturated fat: 7g; Cholesterol: 29mg; Carbohydrates: 26g; Fiber: 3g; Protein: 12g

NEXT DAY This makes a large amount of polenta. Slice firm, refrigerated polenta, and pan fry it in butter until crisp and golden. Serve with eggs, tomato sauce, meat sauce, or chicken and gravy.

PREP
20 MINUTES

COOK
5 MINUTES
ON THE
STOVE TOP
plus
6 HOURS
ON LOW

GLUTEN-FREE

SOY-FREE

NUT-FREE

BUCKWHEAT WITH THREE MUSHROOMS

SERVES 2

Believe it or not, buckwheat is gluten-free. This whole grain is related to rhubarb. Buckwheat groats (also called kasha) are high in fiber and protein and deliciously nutty tasting. So that it doesn't get mushy, we cook the buckwheat with egg in a saucepan before adding it to the slow cooker.

1 cup buckwheat groats

1 egg, beaten

1 onion, chopped

½ cup sliced cremini mushrooms

½ cup sliced button mushrooms

½ cup sliced shiitake mushrooms

2½ cups Vegetable Broth (page 27) or Chicken Stock (page 28)

1 bay leaf

½ teaspoon dried basil leaves

½ teaspoon salt

⅛ teaspoon freshly ground black pepper

1. In a medium bowl, mix the buckwheat groats with the egg, combining well.

2. In a medium saucepan over low heat, sauté the buckwheat mixture until the groats smell toasted, about 5 minutes.

3. In the slow cooker, combine all the ingredients.

4. Cover and cook on low for 5 to 6 hours, or until the buckwheat is tender.

5. Remove and discard the bay leaf, and serve.

PER SERVING Calories: 332; Total fat: 6g; Saturated fat: 2g; Cholesterol: 82mg; Carbohydrates: 56g; Fiber: 8g; Protein: 19g

FARRO PILAF

SERVES 2

PREP
10 MINUTES

COOK
6 HOURS
ON LOW

GLUTEN-FREE

SOY-FREE

NUT-FREE

VEGETARIAN

Farro, a type of wheat used often in Italian cooking, is a whole grain that is considered an ancestor of our modern wheat. It's a good source of protein and iron and can be found at large grocery stores, or you can order it online.

1 cup farro, rinsed

1 onion, chopped

1 cup sliced shiitake mushrooms

1 leek, white part only, chopped

3 garlic cloves, minced

2½ cups Vegetable Broth (page 27)

1 teaspoon dried marjoram leaves

½ teaspoon salt

⅛ teaspoon freshly ground black pepper

2 tablespoons butter

1. In the slow cooker, combine all the ingredients except the butter, and stir.

2. Cover and cook on low for 6 hours, or until the farro is tender.

3. Stir in the butter and serve.

PER SERVING Calories: 586; Total fat: 16g; Saturated fat: 8g; Cholesterol: 31mg; Carbohydrates: 94g; Fiber: 14g; Protein: 23g

PREP
15 MINUTES

COOK
5 HOURS
ON LOW
plus
30 MINUTES
ON HIGH

GLUTEN-FREE

SOY-FREE

NUT-FREE

VEGETARIAN

ASPARAGUS RISOTTO

SERVES 2

This beautiful risotto is made with leeks, garlic, and fresh asparagus. The asparagus is added at the end of the cooking time so that it stays bright green and is crisp-tender.

Nonstick cooking spray

1½ cups Arborio rice

1 leek, white and light green parts only, sliced

2 garlic cloves, minced

¼ cup dry white wine

4 cups Vegetable Broth (page 27)

½ teaspoon salt

⅛ teaspoon freshly ground black pepper

½ pound asparagus

½ cup grated Parmesan cheese

1 tablespoon butter

1. Spray the slow cooker with the nonstick cooking spray.

2. In the slow cooker, combine the rice, leek, garlic, wine, broth, salt, and pepper, and stir.

3. Cover and cook on low for 5 hours, or until the rice is tender. Stir well.

4. Wash and trim the asparagus, and cut it into 1-inch lengths.

5. Add the asparagus to the slow cooker; cover and cook on high for 30 minutes, or until the asparagus is crisp-tender.

6. Stir in the cheese and butter. Cover and let stand for 5 minutes, then serve.

PER SERVING Calories: 813; Total fat: 16g; Saturated fat: 9g; Cholesterol: 36mg; Carbohydrates: 129g; Fiber: 7g; Protein: 32g

PREP IT RIGHT Asparagus will snap naturally where the stalk becomes tender. The ends of asparagus are tough and woody, even after cooking, so snap off the ends and discard, and then rinse the asparagus well and cut it into pieces.

THREE-GRAIN MEDLEY

SERVES 2

PREP
15 MINUTES

COOK
6 MINUTES
ON THE
STOVE TOP
plus
7 HOURS
ON LOW

GLUTEN-FREE

SOY-FREE

NUT-FREE

VEGETARIAN

Some grains are made for the slow cooking environment of the slow cooker. The best choices are whole grains that take a long time to cook on the stove top. Three of those are barley, wild rice, and farro. They combine into a fragrant, elegant pilaf in this easy recipe.

1 tablespoon extra-virgin olive oil

1 onion, chopped

2 garlic cloves, minced

1 carrot, sliced

⅓ cup wild rice, rinsed and drained well

⅓ cup farro, rinsed and drained well

⅓ cup pearl barley, rinsed and drained well

3 cups Vegetable Broth (page 27)

1 bay leaf

½ teaspoon dried basil leaves

½ teaspoon salt

⅛ teaspoon freshly ground black pepper

⅓ cup grated Parmesan cheese

1. In a small saucepan over medium heat, heat the olive oil. Add the onion, garlic, and carrot, and sauté until crisp-tender, about 5 to 6 minutes.

2. In the slow cooker, combine the onion mixture, rice, farro, and barley.

3. Stir in the broth, bay leaf, basil, salt, and pepper.

4. Cover and cook on low for 7 hours, or until the grains are tender. Remove and discard the bay leaf, stir in the cheese, and serve.

PER SERVING Calories: 615; Total fat: 17g; Saturated fat: 6g; Cholesterol: 20mg; Carbohydrates: 90g; Fiber: 14g; Protein: 31g

NEXT DAY This medley is delicious as a filling for an omelet. Beat 5 eggs with ¼ cup cream. Melt 2 tablespoons butter in a nonstick pan. Add the eggs and cook, lifting the edges so uncooked egg flows underneath, until the bottom is set. Add the grain mixture and top with the shredded cheese. Broil until set and then serve.

FOUR-BEAN BAKE

SERVES 2

PREP
20 MINUTES

COOK
15 MINUTES
ON THE
STOVE TOP
plus
8 HOURS
ON LOW
plus
30 MINUTES
ON HIGH

GLUTEN-FREE

SOY-FREE

NUT-FREE

You can switch out the beans in this recipe to suit your needs. If you don't care for lima beans, use navy or cannellini beans instead. Substitute black-eyed peas for the great northern beans, or add a fifth bean! Just keep the proportion of beans and liquid the same.

4 slices bacon

1 onion, chopped

1 cup whole small cremini mushrooms

2 garlic cloves, minced

⅓ cup dried cannellini beans, sorted and rinsed

⅓ cup dried pinto beans, sorted and rinsed

⅓ cup dried great northern beans, sorted and rinsed

⅓ cup dried lima beans, sorted and rinsed

3 cups Vegetable Broth (page 27)

2 tablespoons honey

1 bay leaf

½ teaspoon salt

¼ teaspoon freshly ground black pepper

½ cup tomato sauce

¼ cup whole black olives, pitted

¼ cup chopped fresh flat-leaf parsley

1. In a small skillet over medium-high heat, cook the bacon until crisp, about 10 minutes. Drain the bacon on paper towels, break it into pieces, and refrigerate.

2. In the same pan, sauté the onion in the bacon drippings until crisp-tender, about 5 minutes.

3. In the slow cooker, combine the onion, mushrooms, garlic, all the beans, broth, honey, bay leaf, salt, and pepper.

4. Cover and cook on low for 8 hours.

5. Stir in the tomato sauce and olives. Cover and cook on high for 30 minutes.

6. Remove and discard the bay leaf, garnish with the parsley and bacon, and serve.

PER SERVING Calories: 782; Total fat: 20g; Saturated fat: 6g; Cholesterol: 42mg; Carbohydrates: 103g; Fiber: 25g; Protein: 51g

PREP
20 MINUTES

COOK
15 MINUTES
ON THE
STOVE TOP
plus
9 HOURS
ON LOW

GLUTEN-FREE

SOY-FREE

NUT-FREE

BOSTON BAKED BEANS

SERVES 2

This dish usually uses salt pork, but it can be difficult to find, so we substitute bacon here for the same smoky flavor. This rich recipe is a perfect side dish for meatloaf in the winter. Make sure to cook until the beans are very tender.

3 slices thick bacon

1 onion, chopped

3 garlic cloves, minced

1½ cups dried navy beans, sorted and rinsed

2½ cups water

1 (8-ounce) can tomato sauce

2 tablespoons molasses

2 tablespoons honey

2 tablespoons brown sugar

1 bay leaf

½ teaspoon salt

⅛ teaspoon freshly ground black pepper

1 tablespoon freshly squeezed lemon juice

2 tablespoons Dijon mustard

1. In a small pan over medium-high heat, cook the bacon until crisp, about 10 minutes. Drain the bacon on paper towels and break it into small pieces.

2. In the same pan, cook the onion and garlic in the bacon drippings until tender, about 5 minutes.

3. In the slow cooker, combine the bacon, onion and garlic mixture, beans, water, tomato sauce, molasses, honey, brown sugar, bay leaf, salt, and pepper.

4. Cover and cook on low for 9 hours, or until the beans are very tender.

5. Remove and discard the bay leaf, stir in the lemon juice and mustard, and serve.

PER SERVING Calories: 906; Total fat: 15g; Saturated fat: 4g; Cholesterol: 31mg; Carbohydrates: 150g; Fiber: 42g; Protein: 49g

FRENCH WHITE BEANS WITH THYME

SERVES 2

PREP
10 MINUTES

COOK
7 HOURS
ON LOW

GLUTEN-FREE

SOY-FREE

NUT-FREE

The French usually use flageolet beans, which are small and light green, in this recipe. They can be difficult to find in this country, so we'll substitute great northern beans. Thyme is a classic herb to serve with beans. Cook with the dried form, and finish with fresh chopped thyme.

1 onion, chopped

3 garlic cloves, minced

2 carrots, sliced

1½ cups dried great northern beans, sorted and rinsed

3 cups Chicken Stock (page 28) or Vegetable Broth (page 27)

2 tablespoons extra-virgin olive oil

1 teaspoon salt

½ teaspoon dried thyme leaves

⅛ teaspoon freshly ground black pepper

1 tablespoon minced fresh thyme leaves

⅓ cup grated Parmesan cheese

1. In the slow cooker, combine all the ingredients except the fresh thyme and cheese, and stir.

2. Cover and cook on low for 6 to 7 hours, or until the beans are tender.

3. Stir in the fresh thyme and cheese, and serve.

PER SERVING Calories: 749; Total fat: 23g; Saturated fat: 7g; Cholesterol: 20mg; Carbohydrates: 101g; Fiber: 31g; Protein: 42g

NEXT DAY Leftover beans are delicious puréed and served as a dip, or you can combine them with some rice for a quick lunch. Adding these beans to a green salad turns it into something spectacular, especially when you add some more Parmesan cheese on top (use a vegetable peeler to shave the cheese).

PREP
15 MINUTES

COOK
7 HOURS
ON LOW
plus
30 MINUTES
ON HIGH

SOY-FREE

NUT-FREE

VEGETARIAN

WHOLE-WHEAT PASTA IN TOMATO SAUCE

SERVES 2

The long cooking times of slow cooking make whole-wheat pasta a better choice than durum wheat (semolina) pasta. You can add the pasta at the beginning of the cooking time if you like a very soft pasta, or add it during the last 30 minutes for a more al dente texture.

Nonstick cooking spray

1 onion, chopped

3 garlic cloves, minced

½ cup shredded carrot

2 cups Marinara Sauce (page 36)

1 (14-ounce) can diced tomatoes, undrained

1 cup water

8 ounces uncooked whole-wheat or whole-grain spaghetti pasta

⅓ cup grated Parmesan cheese

1. Spray the slow cooker with the nonstick cooking spray.

2. In the slow cooker, combine all the ingredients except the pasta and cheese, and stir.

3. Cover and cook on low for 7 hours, or until the onions are tender.

4. Break the spaghetti in half and add it to the slow cooker. Make sure that the pasta is covered with the liquid in the slow cooker.

5. Cover and cook on high for 20 to 30 minutes, or until the pasta is tender.

6. Stir, top with the cheese, and serve.

PER SERVING Calories: 765; Total fat: 16g; Saturated fat: 6g; Cholesterol: 25mg; Carbohydrates: 132g; Fiber: 23g; Protein: 34g

DID YOU KNOW? You can substitute other shapes of pasta for spaghetti in this recipe, but those kinds of pasta need a longer cooking time. Penne, ziti, and farfalle will need another 10 minutes or so to cook to al dente.

BBQ BEANS

SERVES 2

PREP
15 MINUTES,
PLUS
OVERNIGHT
TO SOAK

COOK
1 HOUR
ON THE
STOVE TOP
plus
8 HOURS
ON LOW

GLUTEN-FREE

SOY-FREE

NUT-FREE

Because these beans cook in a tomato-based sauce, which is acidic, they should be soaked overnight and parboiled. Acidic ingredients can prevent dried beans from softening enough to be palatable. Parboiling, and cooking for a long time, solves this problem.

½ cup dried black beans, sorted and rinsed

½ cup dried pinto beans, sorted and rinsed

1 teaspoon salt, divided

3 slices bacon

1 onion, chopped

3 garlic cloves, minced

2 cups Chicken Stock (page 28)

1 cup BBQ Sauce (page 40)

2 tablespoons honey

1 tablespoon Dijon mustard

⅛ teaspoon freshly ground black pepper

1. In a medium bowl, cover the beans with water and add ½ teaspoon of salt; cover and let soak overnight.

2. In the morning, drain the beans and rinse them. In a medium saucepan over high heat, cover the beans with water. Bring to a boil; then reduce the heat and simmer the beans for 45 minutes. Drain.

3. In a medium saucepan over medium-high heat, cook the bacon until crisp, about 10 minutes. Remove the bacon and break it into pieces.

4. In the same saucepan over medium-high heat, cook the onion and garlic in the bacon drippings until crisp-tender, about 5 minutes.

5. In the slow cooker, combine all the ingredients.

6. Cover and cook on low for 8 hours, or until the beans are tender, and serve.

PER SERVING Calories: 782; Total fat: 15g; Saturated fat: 4g; Cholesterol: 31mg; Carbohydrates: 131g; Fiber: 17g; Protein: 33g

FARRO WITH SPINACH

SERVES 2

Farro is a delicious side dish, especially when paired with spinach and vegetables. In fact, this hearty recipe makes an excellent vegetarian main dish. The mushrooms give it a "meaty" texture, and the spinach, broth, and cheese make it rich and satisfying.

Nonstick cooking spray

1 leek, white part only, chopped

1 cup sliced cremini mushrooms

2 garlic cloves, minced

1½ cups farro, rinsed

3 cups Vegetable Broth (page 27)

½ teaspoon dried marjoram leaves

½ teaspoon salt

⅛ teaspoon freshly ground black pepper

2 cups baby spinach leaves

⅓ cup grated Parmesan or Romano cheese

1. Spray the slow cooker with the nonstick cooking spray.

2. In the slow cooker, combine all the ingredients except the spinach and cheese, and stir.

3. Cover and cook on low for 6½ hours, or until the farro is almost tender.

4. Stir in the spinach, cover, and cook on low for about 30 minutes more, until the spinach is wilted and the farro is tender.

5. Stir in the cheese and serve.

PER SERVING Calories: 710; Total fat: 12g; Saturated fat: 5g; Cholesterol: 20mg; Carbohydrates: 117g; Fiber: 17g; Protein: 40g

DID YOU KNOW? If you are a vegetarian and are serious about your diet, you should know that many cheeses are made with rennet, which is a part of a cow's stomach. There are vegetarian cheeses made with vegetable rennet; read labels to be sure of what you're buying.

WHEAT BERRY PILAF

PREP
15 MINUTES

COOK
7 HOURS
ON LOW

SOY-FREE

NUT-FREE

VEGETARIAN

MAKES 7 CUPS

Wheat berries are the whole grain of wheat with just the hull removed. You can find them at health food stores and co-ops. They make a deliciously nutty and chewy pilaf.

1 cup wheat berries

1 onion, chopped

1 leek, white part only, chopped

1 cup sliced cremini mushrooms

3 cups Vegetable Broth (page 27)

1 tablespoon freshly squeezed lemon juice

½ teaspoon dried thyme leaves

½ teaspoon salt

⅛ teaspoon freshly ground black pepper

1. Rinse the wheat berries well, and drain.

2. In the slow cooker, combine all the ingredients, and stir.

3. Cover and cook on low for 7 hours, or until the wheat berries and vegetables are tender.

PER SERVING (1 cup) Calories: 65; Total fat: 1g; Saturated fat: 0g; Cholesterol: 0mg; Carbohydrates: 11g; Fiber: 1g; Protein: 4g

PREP
15 MINUTES

COOK
7 HOURS
ON LOW
plus
30 MINUTES
ON HIGH

GLUTEN-FREE

SOY-FREE

NUT-FREE

VEGAN

WHITE BEANS WITH KALE

SERVES 2

Creamy and slightly sweet, white beans are a perfect match for dense, slightly bitter kale. This classic combination is easy to make in the slow cooker. The kale is added during the last half hour, so it keeps some of its chewy texture.

1 onion, chopped

1 leek, white part only, sliced

2 celery stalks, sliced

2 garlic cloves, minced

1 cup dried white lima beans or cannellini beans, sorted and rinsed

2 cups Vegetable Broth (page 27)

½ teaspoon salt

½ teaspoon dried thyme leaves

⅛ teaspoon freshly ground black pepper

3 cups torn kale

1. In the slow cooker, combine all the ingredients except the kale.

2. Cover and cook on low for 7 hours, or until the beans are tender.

3. Add the kale and stir.

4. Cover and cook on high for 30 minutes, or until the kale is tender but still firm, and serve.

PER SERVING Calories: 451; Total fat: 3g; Saturated fat: 1g; Cholesterol: 0mg; Carbohydrates: 80g; Fiber: 27g; Protein: 31g

PREP IT RIGHT To prepare kale, cut out the thick, tough ribs and rinse it well—kale can be sandy, so make sure no grit remains. Then tear the kale into small pieces.

SPICY PINTO BEANS

MAKES 7 CUPS

Pinto beans, so-called for their brown spots that resemble a pinto pony, are great as a side dish for a Mexican meal, or you can use them to make refried beans. See the "Next Day" tip for instructions.

Nonstick cooking spray

1½ cups dried pinto beans, sorted and rinsed

1 onion, chopped

2 garlic cloves, minced

1 jalapeño pepper, minced

1 chipotle pepper in adobo sauce, minced

3½ cups Vegetable Broth (page 27)

1 bay leaf

½ teaspoon salt

⅛ teaspoon freshly ground black pepper

⅛ teaspoon ground cayenne pepper

1. Spray the slow cooker with the nonstick cooking spray.

2. In the slow cooker, combine all the ingredients.

3. Cover and cook on low for 7 to 8 hours, or until the beans are very tender.

4. Remove and discard the bay leaf, and serve.

PER SERVING (1 cup) Calories: 176; Total fat: 1g; Saturated fat: 0g; Cholesterol: 0mg; Carbohydrates: 29g; Fiber: 7g; Protein: 12g

NEXT DAY To make refried beans, heat 2 tablespoons oil, bacon drippings, or butter in a large skillet over medium heat. Add the bean mixture, and mash with the back of a spoon. Cook and stir until the mixture is hot and thickened, and serve.

GREEK CHICKPEAS

SERVES 2

Chickpeas, also called garbanzo beans, are round legumes with a nutty taste and tender texture. Here, they're paired with flavors of Greece—lemon, feta, rosemary, and oregano—whose bright flavors perfectly complement the nuttiness of chickpeas.

Nonstick cooking spray

1 onion, chopped

2 garlic cloves, minced

1½ cups dried chickpeas, sorted and rinsed

4 cups Chicken Stock (page 28) or Vegetable Broth (page 27)

1 sprig fresh rosemary

½ teaspoon dried oregano leaves

½ teaspoon salt

⅛ teaspoon freshly ground black pepper

½ cup crumbled feta cheese

2 tablespoons freshly squeezed lemon juice

½ teaspoon lemon zest

1. Spray the slow cooker with the nonstick cooking spray.

2. In the slow cooker, combine the onion, garlic, chickpeas, stock, rosemary, oregano, salt, and pepper.

3. Cover and cook on low for 8 to 9 hours, or until the chickpeas are tender. Drain if necessary.

4. Add the feta, lemon juice, and lemon zest, and serve.

PER SERVING Calories: 701; Total fat: 19g; Saturated fat: 7g; Cholesterol: 33mg; Carbohydrates: 101g; Fiber: 28g; Protein: 37g

NEXT DAY The leftovers from this recipe are delicious in hummus, a healthy and flavorful appetizer spread or dip. Combine 2 cups of the cooked chickpea mixture in a blender or food processor with ½ cup tahini, 3 tablespoons extra-virgin olive oil, and 1 tablespoon freshly squeezed lemon juice. Blend or process until smooth, and serve.

PREP
20 MINUTES

COOK
8 HOURS
ON LOW

GLUTEN-FREE

SOY-FREE

NUT-FREE

VEGAN

SPICY BLACK BEANS WITH ROOT VEGGIES

SERVES 2

Suspend your disbelief as your slow cooker works its magic, rendering the dried black beans and root vegetables unbelievably tender and flavorful. Serve the dish with a simple roast chicken for a well-rounded dinner.

1 onion, chopped

1 leek, white part only, sliced

3 garlic cloves, minced

1 jalapeño pepper, minced

2 Yukon Gold potatoes, peeled and cubed

1 parsnip, peeled and cubed

1 carrot, sliced

1 cup dried black beans, sorted and rinsed

2 cups Vegetable Broth (page 27)

2 teaspoons chili powder

½ teaspoon dried marjoram leaves

½ teaspoon salt

⅛ teaspoon freshly ground black pepper

⅛ teaspoon crushed red pepper flakes

1. In the slow cooker, combine all the ingredients.

2. Cover and cook on low for 7 to 8 hours, or until the beans and vegetables are tender, and serve.

PER SERVING Calories: 627; Total fat: 4g; Saturated fat: 1g; Cholesterol: 0mg; Carbohydrates: 122g; Fiber: 24g; Protein: 32g

TUSCAN CHICKPEAS WITH GREENS

SERVES 2

PREP
15 MINUTES

COOK
6 MINUTES
ON THE
STOVE TOP
plus
8½ HOURS
ON LOW

GLUTEN-FREE

SOY-FREE

NUT-FREE

VEGETARIAN

The flavors of Tuscany—rosemary, oregano, tomatoes, and Parmesan cheese—round out the nutty chickpeas in this hearty dish. Serve it with grilled steak, roasted pork, or a roast chicken for a satisfying dinner.

1 tablespoon extra-virgin olive oil

1 onion, chopped

4 garlic cloves, minced

1½ cups dried chickpeas, sorted and rinsed

3½ cups Vegetable Broth (page 27)

1 sprig fresh rosemary

1 teaspoon dried oregano leaves

1 teaspoon lemon zest

1 teaspoon salt

⅛ teaspoon freshly ground black pepper

2 cups chopped kale

1 cup chopped Swiss chard

1 large tomato, seeded and chopped

½ cup grated Parmesan cheese

1. In a small saucepan over medium heat, heat the olive oil. Add the onion and garlic and sauté, stirring, until tender, about 6 minutes.

2. In the slow cooker, combine the onion and garlic mixture, chickpeas, broth, rosemary, oregano, lemon zest, salt, and pepper.

3. Cover and cook on low for 8 hours, or until the chickpeas are tender.

4. Stir in the kale, Swiss chard, and tomato. Cover and cook on low for 30 minutes more, or until the greens are tender. Stir in the cheese and serve.

PER SERVING Calories: 853; Total fat: 25g; Saturated fat: 7g; Cholesterol: 20mg; Carbohydrates: 113g; Fiber: 30g; Protein: 51g

NINE

VEGETABLES & SIDES

There's no way around it—when you have only one size of slow cooker, yields will be higher for dishes that are not mains. Why? Because you have to put in a minimum of ingredients to make sure the appliance cooks correctly. With a 3- to 3½-quart slow cooker, side dishes will produce more food than you'll want to eat in one night. As a result, these recipes are really best made for entertaining, or if you don't mind a little freezing here and there.

SCALLOPED POTATOES

PREP
20 MINUTES

COOK
1 MINUTE
ON THE
STOVE TOP
plus
7 HOURS
ON LOW

MAKES 9 (¾-CUP) SERVINGS

The potatoes here are delicious, creamy, and perfectly tender.
A great side for the holidays, these potatoes will happily make
themselves while you tend to other things.

GLUTEN-FREE

SOY-FREE

NUT-FREE

VEGETARIAN

Nonstick cooking spray

3 large russet potatoes, peeled and thinly sliced

1 onion, finely chopped

3 garlic cloves, minced

1 teaspoon dried basil leaves

1 teaspoon salt

⅛ teaspoon freshly ground black pepper

1 cup grated Havarti cheese

½ cup grated white Cheddar cheese

½ cup light cream

½ cup heavy cream

2 tablespoons butter

⅓ cup grated Parmesan cheese

1. Spray the slow cooker with the nonstick cooking spray.

2. In the slow cooker, layer the potatoes, onion, garlic, basil, salt, pepper, Havarti cheese, and Cheddar cheese, making about 4 layers.

3. In a small saucepan over high heat, heat the light cream, heavy cream, and butter until the butter melts, about a minute. Pour the mixture into the slow cooker, and sprinkle with the Parmesan cheese.

4. Cover and cook on low for 7 hours, or until the potatoes are tender, and serve.

PER SERVING Calories: 240; Total fat: 14g; Saturated fat: 9g; Cholesterol: 45mg; Carbohydrates: 22g; Fiber: 3g; Protein: 9g

NEXT DAY Nothing is better than leftover scalloped potatoes. Heat them in a saucepan or in the microwave, or you can make a delicious dish of scalloped potatoes and ham. Just mix them in a small casserole dish, add some more cream and cheese, bake at 350°F until bubbly, and serve.

GREEN BEANS AND POTATOES

MAKES 9 (¾-CUP) SERVINGS

The beans and potatoes become very tender and absorb heady, aromatic flavor from the onion and garlic. If you like, add some cooked bacon to the recipe for an irresistible smokiness.

Nonstick cooking spray

1 onion, chopped

2 garlic cloves, minced

1 leek, white part only, sliced thin

2 cups whole fresh green string beans

3 cups small creamer potatoes

½ cup Vegetable Broth (page 27)

2 tablespoons freshly squeezed lemon juice

½ teaspoon salt

½ teaspoon dried thyme leaves

⅛ teaspoon freshly ground black pepper

1. Spray the slow cooker with the nonstick cooking spray.

2. In the slow cooker, combine all the ingredients.

3. Cover and cook on low for 5 to 6 hours, or until the potatoes and beans are tender, and serve.

PER SERVING Calories: 74; Total fat: 0g; Saturated fat: 0g; Cholesterol: 0mg; Carbohydrates: 17g; Fiber: 5g; Protein: 3g

NEXT DAY Use any leftovers to make this delicious potato salad. Mix ⅓ cup mayonnaise, 2 tablespoons plain yogurt, 1 tablespoon freshly squeezed lemon juice, and 1 teaspoon fresh thyme leaves in a bowl. Stir in 2 cups leftover Green Beans and Potatoes, and then cover and chill for a few hours before serving.

CHEESY HASH BROWNS

PREP
10 MINUTES

COOK
7 HOURS
ON LOW
plus
1 MINUTE
ON THE
STOVE TOP

GLUTEN-FREE

SOY-FREE

NUT-FREE

VEGETARIAN

MAKES 9 (¾-CUP) SERVINGS

Excellent quality hash brown potatoes are sold prepared in the freezer section of the supermarket. If you prefer, you can make your own hash (see the "Prep It Right" tip). The end result is creamy, cheesy, rich, and so delicious.

Nonstick cooking spray

1 (20-ounce) package frozen hash brown potatoes

1 onion, finely chopped

3 garlic cloves, minced

1 cup grated Colby or Gruyère cheese

1 cup milk

⅓ cup heavy cream

3 tablespoons butter

½ teaspoon dried marjoram leaves

¼ teaspoon salt

⅛ teaspoon freshly ground black pepper

½ cup sour cream

1. Spray the slow cooker with the nonstick cooking spray.

2. In the slow cooker, combine the hash brown potatoes, onion, and garlic, and stir. Mix in the cheese.

3. In a small saucepan over high heat, combine the milk, cream, butter, marjoram, salt, and pepper, and heat until the butter melts, about a minute. Remove from the heat and stir in the sour cream.

4. Pour the milk mixture into the slow cooker.

5. Cover and cook on low for 7 hours, or until the potatoes are tender, and serve.

PER SERVING Calories: 320; Total fat: 22g; Saturated fat: 10g; Cholesterol: 40mg; Carbohydrates: 26g; Fiber: 2g; Protein: 6g

PREP IT RIGHT If you want to use fresh potatoes to make this recipe from scratch, scrub four large russet potatoes and peel them. Shred them on a coarse grater directly into a bowl of ice water to help keep the potatoes from turning brown. Dry the potatoes thoroughly in a clean kitchen towel, and use as directed.

GLUTEN-FREE

SOY-FREE

NUT-FREE

VEGETARIAN

GLAZED CITRUS CARROTS

MAKES 9 (¾-CUP) SERVINGS

Sweet carrots and honey contrast with tart lemon juice and zest, and sweet-citrusy orange juice and zest, to make a spectacular dish that may outshine your main course!

1½ pounds whole small carrots

1 leek, white part only, sliced

3 garlic cloves, minced

¼ cup Vegetable Broth (page 27) or water

2 tablespoons freshly squeezed lemon juice

2 tablespoons orange juice

2 tablespoons honey

½ teaspoon lemon zest

½ teaspoon orange zest

½ teaspoon salt

⅛ teaspoon freshly ground black pepper

1. Peel the carrots and cut off the roots. Trim off the tops, if the carrots have them. Put the carrots in the slow cooker.

2. Add the leek and garlic, and stir. Then add all the remaining ingredients and stir.

3. Cover and cook on low for 7 to 8 hours, or until the carrots are tender.

PER SERVING Calories: 56; Total fat: 0g; Saturated fat: 0g; Cholesterol: 0mg; Carbohydrates: 14g; Fiber: 2g; Protein: 1g

BROWN RICE AND VEGETABLE PILAF

MAKES 9 (¾-CUP) SERVINGS

Nutty brown rice together with meaty mushrooms, sweet carrots, and creamy Parmesan add lots of flavor and color to this simple side. Pilaf is not only a delicious side but a great lunch when served with some warm bread.

1 onion, minced

1 cup sliced cremini mushrooms

2 carrots, sliced

2 garlic cloves, minced

1½ cups long-grain brown rice

2½ cups Vegetable Broth (page 27)

½ teaspoon salt

½ teaspoon dried marjoram leaves

⅛ teaspoon freshly ground black pepper

⅓ cup grated Parmesan cheese

1. In the slow cooker, combine the onion, mushrooms, carrots, garlic, and rice.

2. Add the broth, salt, marjoram, and pepper, and stir.

3. Cover and cook on low for 5 hours, or until the rice is tender and the liquid is absorbed.

4. Stir in the cheese and serve.

PER SERVING Calories: 145; Total fat: 2g; Saturated fat: 1g; Cholesterol: 5mg; Carbohydrates: 26g; Fiber: 2g; Protein: 6g

NEXT DAY Leftover pilaf can be made into crisp rice cakes. Combine 2 cups of the pilaf with 1 beaten egg and ½ cup shredded Cheddar cheese. Form into patties and refrigerate for 30 minutes. Fry in hot extra-virgin olive oil, turning once, until crisp and brown, and serve.

ROOT VEGETABLE HASH

MAKES 9 (¾-CUP) SERVINGS

A hash is a combination of ingredients that are chopped to about the same size, usually cooked on the stove top until crisp. But hash can also be a mélange of vegetables and fruits slowly cooked until tender. This wonderful and unusual recipe is delicious.

4 carrots, peeled and cut into 1-inch cubes

3 large russet potatoes, peeled and cut into 1-inch cubes

1 onion, diced

3 garlic cloves, minced

½ teaspoon salt

⅛ teaspoon freshly ground black pepper

½ teaspoon dried thyme leaves

1 sprig rosemary

½ cup Vegetable Broth (page 27)

3 plums, cut into 1-inch pieces

1. In the slow cooker, combine the carrots, potatoes, onion, and garlic. Sprinkle with the salt, pepper, and thyme, and stir.

2. Imbed the rosemary sprig in the vegetables.

3. Pour the broth over everything.

4. Cover and cook on low for 7½ hours, or until the vegetables are tender.

5. Stir in the plums, cover, and cook on low for 30 minutes, until tender.

6. Remove and discard the rosemary sprig, and serve.

PER SERVING Calories: 112; Total fat: 0g; Saturated fat: 0g; Cholesterol: 0mg; Carbohydrates: 25g; Fiber: 4g; Protein: 3g

SEASONAL SUBSTITUTION Although many people don't use root vegetables such as parsnips, rutabagas, and turnips, they are delicious, inexpensive, and plentiful at the supermarket. Try them in this hash in place of the carrots and potatoes in the winter, when they are abundant. You won't be disappointed.

GLUTEN-FREE

SOY-FREE

NUT-FREE

VEGETARIAN

RATATOUILLE

MAKES 9 (¾-CUP) SERVINGS

Ratatouille is a combination of vegetables that are cooked together slowly so the flavors blend and the veggies become very tender. It can be made in many ways; this version is easy and inexpensive. The flavors in this veggie combo meld and blend while slow-cooking their way to a healthy, delicious side dish.

Nonstick cooking spray

1 onion, chopped

3 garlic cloves, sliced

1 eggplant, cut into 1-inch pieces

2 carrots, peeled and cut into chunks

1 cup sliced cremini mushrooms

2 large tomatoes, seeded and chopped

1 tablespoon extra-virgin olive oil

¼ cup tomato paste

1 (8-ounce) can tomato sauce

1 teaspoon salt

½ teaspoon dried basil leaves

½ teaspoon dried thyme leaves

¼ teaspoon freshly ground black pepper

1 bay leaf

½ cup grated Parmesan cheese

1. Spray the slow cooker with the nonstick cooking spray.

2. In the slow cooker, combine the onion, garlic, eggplant, carrots, mushrooms, and tomatoes. Drizzle the olive oil over everything.

3. In a small bowl, mix the tomato paste, tomato sauce, salt, basil, thyme, and pepper to dissolve the tomato paste. Pour the mixture into the slow cooker and add the bay leaf.

4. Cover and cook on low for 8 hours, until the vegetables are tender.

5. Remove and discard the bay leaf, stir in the Parmesan cheese, and serve.

PER SERVING Calories: 61; Total fat: 2g; Saturated fat: 0g; Cholesterol: 0mg; Carbohydrates: 11g; Fiber: 4g; Protein: 2g

HARVARD BEETS

MAKES 9 (¾-CUP) SERVINGS

So-called because Harvard football jerseys are the same deep crimson color of this root vegetable, this yummy recipe has a gorgeous sweet-sour balance that you'll crave.

1½ pounds small beets, peeled and thickly sliced

1 onion, chopped

3 garlic cloves, sliced

½ cup brown sugar

2 tablespoons cornstarch

⅓ cup orange juice

3 tablespoons freshly squeezed lemon juice

2 tablespoons honey

2 tablespoons butter

½ teaspoon salt

¼ teaspoon ground cinnamon

1. In the slow cooker, combine the beets, onion, and garlic.

2. In a medium bowl, mix the brown sugar, cornstarch, orange juice, lemon juice, and honey until well combined. Pour the mixture into the slow cooker.

3. Dot the top of the ingredients in the slow cooker with the butter, and sprinkle with the salt and cinnamon.

4. Cover and cook on low for 8 hours, or until the beets are tender, and serve.

PER SERVING Calories: 119; Total fat: 3g; Saturated fat: 2g; Cholesterol: 7mg; Carbohydrates: 23g; Fiber: 3g; Protein: 2g

NEXT DAY Leftovers are perfect for a cold borscht. The soup will be sweet (because of the beets), so it's perfect as an appetizer. Purée the beets with light cream in a blender or food processor. Taste, correct the seasoning, and chill until serving time.

SPICY CREAMER POTATOES

MAKES 7 (1-CUP) SERVINGS

Creamer potatoes are tiny new potatoes with a light yellow skin. They are sometimes sold in boxes in the produce section of the supermarket. They usually cook quickly, but adding an acid (lemon juice in this case) here ensures they slowly cook their way to creamy deliciousness.

2 pounds creamer potatoes

1 onion, chopped

3 garlic cloves, minced

1 chipotle chile in adobo sauce, minced

2 tablespoons freshly squeezed lemon juice

2 tablespoons water

1 tablespoon chili powder

½ teaspoon ground cumin

½ teaspoon salt

⅛ teaspoon freshly ground black pepper

1. In the slow cooker, combine all the ingredients and stir.

2. Cover and cook on low for 7 to 8 hours, or until the potatoes are tender, and serve.

PER SERVING Calories: 102; Total fat: 0g; Saturated fat: 0g; Cholesterol: 0mg; Carbohydrates: 24g; Fiber: 4g; Protein: 2g

NEXT DAY Leftover cooked potatoes are delicious made into a hash the next day. Coarsely chop the potatoes. Melt some butter in a skillet and add the potatoes. Cook over medium heat, stirring occasionally, until the potatoes are crisp and brown. You can top this with a fried egg for another easy meal.

CURRIED ROASTED VEGETABLES

MAKES 9 (¾-CUP) SERVINGS

PREP
20 MINUTES

COOK
7 HOURS
ON LOW

GLUTEN-FREE

SOY-FREE

NUT-FREE

VEGETARIAN

Vegetables roasted in the slow cooker become very sweet and tender. They are softer than veggies roasted in the oven, but they have more flavor. Serve this recipe with roasted chicken.

Nonstick cooking spray

3 carrots, cut into chunks

1 onion, chopped

2 red bell peppers, cut into strips

2 sweet potatoes, cubed

6 garlic cloves, sliced

2 tablespoons extra-virgin olive oil

1 teaspoon salt

2 teaspoons curry powder or Curry Rub (page 23)

⅛ teaspoon freshly ground black pepper

2 tablespoons butter

1. Spray the slow cooker with the nonstick cooking spray.

2. In the slow cooker, combine the carrots, onion, bell peppers, sweet potatoes, and garlic, and stir. Drizzle with the olive oil; sprinkle with the salt, curry powder, and pepper; and stir.

3. Cover and cook on low for 7 hours, or until the vegetables are tender. If you're at home while the veggies are cooking, stir occasionally.

4. Add the butter, toss gently, and serve.

PER SERVING Calories: 115; Total fat: 6g; Saturated fat: 2g; Cholesterol: 7mg; Carbohydrates: 15g; Fiber: 3g; Protein: 1g

MASHED SWEET POTATOES WITH GARLIC

MAKES 7 (1-CUP) SERVINGS

Mashed sweet potatoes are a nice change of pace from mashed white potatoes. They are also much healthier: Sweet potatoes are loaded with vitamin A. This easy recipe is scented with garlic, which becomes sweet and nutty when cooked for a long time. Garnish with fried sage for a little crunch and a delicious complementary flavor.

Nonstick cooking spray

4 large sweet potatoes, peeled and cubed

1 onion, chopped

6 garlic cloves, peeled

½ cup orange juice

2 tablespoons honey

1 teaspoon salt

⅛ teaspoon freshly ground black pepper

⅓ cup butter, at room temperature

½ cup heavy cream

1. Spray the slow cooker with the nonstick cooking spray.

2. In the slow cooker, combine the sweet potatoes, onion, and garlic.

3. Pour the orange juice and honey over everything, and stir. Sprinkle with the salt and pepper.

4. Cover and cook on low for 8 hours, or until the potatoes are tender.

5. Add the butter and cream, mash using a potato masher or immersion blender, and serve.

PER SERVING Calories: 306; Total fat: 13g; Saturated fat: 8g; Cholesterol: 38mg; Carbohydrates: 45g; Fiber: 6g; Protein: 3g

NEXT DAY Leftover mashed sweet potatoes make the most incredible potato cakes. Mix 2 cups leftover potatoes with 1 beaten egg and ½ cup bread crumbs. Form into cakes and coat in flour. Fry in butter until golden brown on both sides, and serve.

CARAMELIZED ONIONS AND GARLIC

MAKES 6 (½-CUP) SERVINGS

Caramelized onions and garlic are delicious on their own, but they are also fabulous added to many recipes. Freeze this recipe in ½-cup portions and add to stews, casseroles, chili, risotto, and soups. It's also delicious as a sandwich spread or a garnish for roast chicken.

5 large onions, sliced

12 garlic cloves, peeled

2 tablespoons extra-virgin olive oil

1 tablespoon butter

½ teaspoon salt

1. Spray the slow cooker with the nonstick cooking spray.

2. In the slow cooker, combine all the ingredients and stir.

3. Cover and cook on low for 9 hours, until the onions and garlic are golden brown. If you're at home during the day, stir occasionally.

4. Serve.

PER SERVING Calories: 116; Total fat: 7g; Saturated fat: 2g; Cholesterol: 5mg; Carbohydrates: 14g; Fiber: 3g; Protein: 2g

APRICOT–CHESTNUT STUFFING

PREP
20 MINUTES

COOK
5 MINUTES
ON THE
STOVE TOP
plus
8 HOURS
ON LOW

SOY-FREE

VEGETARIAN

MAKES 10 (¾-CUP) SERVINGS

The slow cooker is one of the best, most stress-free ways to make stuffing for the holidays. The moist environment of the slow cooker mimics the inside of the turkey, so this recipe is simply perfect. Any leftovers freeze nicely.

Nonstick cooking spray

3 tablespoons butter

1 onion, chopped

1 leek, white part only, chopped

3 garlic cloves, minced

1 (16-ounce) can whole peeled chestnuts, chopped

⅔ cup chopped dried apricots

½ cup chopped walnuts

8 slices whole-wheat bread, cut into 1-inch cubes

2 eggs, beaten

¼ cup milk

¼ cup Vegetable Broth (page 27)

1 teaspoon salt

½ teaspoon dried thyme leaves

½ teaspoon dried basil leaves

⅛ teaspoon freshly ground black pepper

1. Spray the slow cooker with the nonstick cooking spray.

2. In a medium saucepan over medium heat, melt the butter. Add the onion, leek, and garlic, and sauté, stirring, until tender, about 5 minutes. Add the mixture to the slow cooker.

3. Add the chestnuts, apricots, walnuts, and bread.

4. In a small bowl, beat the eggs with the milk, broth, salt, thyme, basil, and pepper. Pour the mixture into the slow cooker and stir.

5. Cover and cook on low for 7 to 8 hours, or until the stuffing registers 165°F on a food thermometer, and serve.

PER SERVING Calories: 209; Total fat: 9g; Saturated fat: 3g; Cholesterol: 42g Carbohydrates: 25g; Fiber: 5g; Protein: 7g

NEXT DAY You can use leftover stuffing to make crisp patties that you can top with reheated turkey or ham and gravy. Combine 2 cups leftover stuffing with 1 egg, and form into patties. Brown in melted butter until crisp and golden brown.

PREP
20 MINUTES

COOK
6 MINUTES
ON THE
STOVE TOP
plus
8 HOURS
ON LOW

SOY-FREE

NUT-FREE

VEGETARIAN

PUMPERNICKEL–CRANBERRY STUFFING

MAKES 10 (¾-CUP) SERVINGS

Stuffing can be made out of just about any combination of bread or grain and vegetables or fruit. This recipe is hearty and well flavored, with pumpernickel bread and dried cranberries. It's delicious served with roast turkey, chicken, or beef. The leftovers freeze beautifully.

2 tablespoons butter

1 tablespoon extra-virgin olive oil

1 onion, chopped

1 cup sliced celery stalk

3 garlic cloves, sliced

Nonstick cooking spray

1 cup dried cranberries

6 cups (1-inch cubes) pumpernickel bread

1 egg, beaten

½ cup Vegetable Broth (page 27)

1 teaspoon fennel seeds

1 teaspoon salt

¼ teaspoon freshly ground black pepper

1. In a medium saucepan over medium heat, melt the butter and olive oil. Add the onion, celery, and garlic, and sauté, stirring, until tender, about 6 minutes.

2. Spray the slow cooker with the nonstick cooking spray.

3. In the slow cooker, stir together the onion mixture, cranberries, and bread cubes.

4. In a small bowl, beat the egg, broth, fennel seeds, salt, and pepper. Pour the mixture into the slow cooker and stir.

5. Cover and cook on low for 7 to 8 hours, or until the stuffing registers 165°F on a food thermometer, and serve.

PER SERVING Calories: 72; Total fat: 5g; Saturated fat: 2g; Cholesterol: 22mg; Carbohydrates: 9g; Fiber: 1g; Protein: 2g

NEXT DAY Leftover stuffing makes an excellent hash. Cook it in melted butter until crisp and brown, and then serve topped with a poached egg.

CURRIED CAULIFLOWER AND CARROTS

PREP
20 MINUTES

COOK
8 HOURS
ON LOW

GLUTEN-FREE

SOY-FREE

NUT-FREE

VEGAN

MAKES 9 (¾-CUP) SERVINGS

This cruciferous vegetable is delicious and so good for you. It contains compounds that may help fight cancer, has anti-inflammatory compounds, and can even improve blood pressure.

Nonstick cooking spray

1 onion, chopped

2 garlic cloves, minced

1 tablespoon grated fresh ginger

1 tablespoon Curry Rub (page 23)

1 head cauliflower, broken into florets

2½ cups baby carrots

½ cup Vegetable Broth (page 27)

½ teaspoon salt

⅛ teaspoon freshly ground black pepper

1. Spray the slow cooker with the nonstick cooking spray.

2. In the slow cooker, combine all the ingredients and stir.

3. Cover and cook on low for 8 hours, or until the vegetables are tender, and serve.

PER SERVING Calories: 40; Total fat: 0g; Saturated fat: 0g; Cholesterol: 0mg; Carbohydrates: 8g; Fiber: 3g; Protein: 1g

PERFECT PAIR This spicy dish is delicious served with a grilled steak, pork chops, or chicken. Add a green salad tossed with sliced mushrooms for a wonderfully easy meal.

TEN

BREAKFASTS

Cooking breakfast in the slow cooker means you get to wake up to a delicious meal that is ready to eat. In fact, the aroma of the food cooking will probably wake you up! Granola, oatmeal, stratas, and egg bakes work very well in the slow cooker. A crustless quiche and some French toast round out this savory and sweet collection. Most of these recipes cook for 6 hours on low; use the keep-warm setting to stretch that to 8 hours.

PREP
10 MINUTES

COOK
2 MINUTES
ON THE
STOVE TOP
plus
7 HOURS
ON LOW

NUTTY OATMEAL

MAKES 7 CUPS

This oatmeal, with its nutty-sweet notes, goes perfectly with bacon and your morning beverage of choice. Who says oatmeal is boring?

1 cup chopped walnuts

Nonstick cooking spray

2 cups rolled oats (not instant or quick cooking)

1 cup raisins

3 cups almond milk

1½ cups apple juice

⅓ cup honey

⅓ cup brown sugar

½ teaspoon ground cinnamon

¼ teaspoon ground nutmeg

¼ teaspoon salt

1. In a small saucepan over medium-low heat, toast the walnuts until fragrant, about 2 minutes, stirring frequently.

2. Spray the slow cooker with the nonstick cooking spray.

3. In the slow cooker, combine the walnuts, oats, and raisins.

4. In a large bowl, beat the almond milk, apple juice, honey, brown sugar, cinnamon, nutmeg, and salt. Pour the mixture into the slow cooker.

5. Cover and cook on low for 7 hours, or until the oatmeal is thickened and tender, and serve.

PER SERVING (1 cup) Calories: 384; Total fat: 13g; Saturated fat: 1g; Cholesterol: 0mg; Carbohydrates: 63g; Fiber: 5g; Protein: 9g

NEXT DAY Make fried oatmeal the next morning! Refrigerate any leftovers in a glass baking dish. In the morning, slice the firm oatmeal, and cook it on both sides in melted butter. Top with maple syrup and dig in.

PREP
15 MINUTES

COOK
ABOUT
5 MINUTES
ON THE
STOVE TOP
plus
4 HOURS
ON LOW

SOY-FREE

VEGETARIAN

GRANOLA

MAKES 8 CUPS

Nuts, seeds, coconut, sweet honey, vanilla, and cinnamon meld for a perfectly crunchy breakfast. Homemade granola tastes so much better than any packaged variety, no matter how fresh.

Nonstick cooking spray

4 cups old-fashioned rolled oats

1 cup slivered almonds

1 cup coarsely chopped pecans

1 cup sunflower seeds

1 cup shredded coconut

⅓ cup butter or coconut oil

2 tablespoons safflower oil

½ cup honey

⅓ cup brown sugar

2 teaspoons vanilla

1 teaspoon ground cinnamon

½ teaspoon salt

1. Spray the slow cooker with the nonstick cooking spray.

2. In the slow cooker, combine the oats, almonds, pecans, sunflower seeds, and coconut.

3. In a medium saucepan over low heat, heat the butter, safflower oil, honey, brown sugar, vanilla, cinnamon, and salt until the butter melts, about 5 minutes.

4. Drizzle the butter mixture over the ingredients in the slow cooker and stir to coat.

5. Cover, but leave the lid slightly ajar, and cook on low for 3 to 4 hours, stirring every hour if possible, until the mixture is golden brown.

6. Remove the granola to greased baking sheets and spread into an even layer. Let cool, and then break into pieces. Serve or store in an airtight container at room temperature.

PER SERVING (1 cup) Calories: 525; Total fat: 31g; Saturated fat: 10g; Cholesterol: 23mg; Carbohydrates: 57g; Fiber: 8g; Protein: 10g

PREP IT RIGHT You can customize this recipe to your tastes. Add more cinnamon, use nutmeg instead, add different nuts, or add dried fruit after the granola is done cooking and has cooled.

FRUITY STEEL-CUT OATMEAL

SERVES 2

Steel-cut oats are different from rolled oats. The steel-cut oats are whole oat groats that are chopped into pieces, while rolled oats have been steamed and rolled into flat flakes. The steel-cut oats take much longer to cook, but the result can't be beat.

Nonstick cooking spray

1½ cups steel-cut oats

½ cup dried cranberries

½ cup golden raisins

½ cup chopped dried apricots

5 cups water

1 cup almond milk

3 tablespoons brown sugar

2 tablespoons honey

½ teaspoon salt

2 teaspoons vanilla

1. Spray the slow cooker with the nonstick cooking spray.

2. In the slow cooker, combine the oats, cranberries, raisins, and apricots, and stir.

3. Add the water, almond milk, brown sugar, honey, salt, and vanilla, and stir.

4. Cover and cook on low for 7½ hours, or until the oats are creamy, and serve.

PER SERVING Calories: 758; Total fat: 9g; Saturated fat: 2g; Cholesterol: 0mg; Carbohydrates: 148g; Fiber: 16g; Protein: 20g

PERFECT PAIR This dish is excellent served with maple syrup or honey and toasted nuts. Or you can pour some cold cream or milk over the hot oatmeal.

VEGGIE HASH WITH EGGS

SERVES 2

You can poach eggs very successfully in the slow cooker. Just make indentations into the hash mixture, and slip in the eggs. Cover and cook for about 10 to 15 minutes, or until the eggs are set.

Nonstick cooking spray

1 onion, chopped

2 garlic cloves, minced

1 red bell pepper, chopped

1 yellow summer squash, chopped

2 carrots, chopped

2 Yukon Gold potatoes, peeled and chopped

2 large tomatoes, seeded and chopped

¼ cup Vegetable Broth (page 27)

½ teaspoon salt

⅛ teaspoon freshly ground black pepper

½ teaspoon dried thyme leaves

3 or 4 eggs

½ teaspoon ground sweet paprika

1. Spray the slow cooker with the nonstick cooking spray.

2. In the slow cooker, combine all the ingredients except the eggs and paprika, and stir.

3. Cover and cook on low for 6 hours.

4. Uncover and make 1 indentation in the vegetable mixture for each egg. Break 1 egg into a small cup and slip the egg into an indentation. Repeat with the remaining eggs. Sprinkle with the paprika.

5. Cover and cook on low for 10 to 15 minutes, or until the eggs are just set, and serve.

PER SERVING Calories: 351; Total fat: 8g; Saturated fat: 2g; Cholesterol: 246mg; Carbohydrates: 58g; Fiber: 10g; Protein: 17g

DID YOU KNOW? Unless the eggs you use are pasteurized, cooking them less than well-done can be unsafe, particularly if you are elderly or have a compromised immune system. Cook the eggs until the whites and yolks are set, or they register 160°F on a food thermometer.

EGG-POTATO BAKE

SERVES 2

PREP
20 MINUTES

COOK
15 MINUTES
ON THE
STOVE TOP
plus
6 HOURS
ON LOW

Eggs, potatoes, sausage, and cheese combine to make a kind of frittata that is satisfying and hearty; perfect for a cold winter morning.

GLUTEN-FREE

SOY-FREE

NUT-FREE

2 slices bacon, chopped

1 cup pork sausage

1 onion, chopped

1 cup sliced button mushrooms

2 garlic cloves, minced

1 orange bell pepper, chopped

Nonstick cooking spray

3 russet potatoes, peeled and sliced

1 cup shredded Havarti cheese

½ cup shredded Colby cheese

5 eggs, beaten

1 cup milk

½ teaspoon salt

½ teaspoon dried thyme leaves

⅛ teaspoon freshly ground black pepper

1. In a medium skillet over medium heat, cook the bacon and sausage until the bacon is crisp and the sausage is browned, 10 minutes or so, stirring frequently. Remove the bacon and sausage to a paper towel–lined plate to drain. Remove and discard all but 1 tablespoon of drippings from the pan.

2. In the same skillet over medium heat, cook the onion, mushrooms, and garlic in the remaining drippings until tender, about 5 minutes. Remove from the heat and add the bell pepper, bacon, and sausage.

3. Line the slow cooker with heavy-duty foil and spray with the nonstick cooking spray.

4. In the slow cooker, layer the potatoes, bacon mixture, and cheeses.

5. In a medium bowl, beat the eggs, milk, salt, thyme, and pepper. Pour the egg mixture into the slow cooker.

6. Cover and cook on low for 6 hours, or until the temperature reaches 160°F on a food thermometer.

7. Using the foil, remove from the slow cooker, cut into squares, and serve.

PER SERVING Calories: 1011; Total fat: 56g; Saturated fat: 26g; Cholesterol: 546mg; Carbohydrates: 71g; Fiber: 11g; Protein: 58g

THREE-CHEESE VEGETABLE STRATA

SERVES 2

PREP
20 MINUTES

COOK
10 MINUTES
ON THE
STOVE TOP
plus
6 HOURS
ON LOW

SOY-FREE

NUT-FREE

Cubes of light French bread layered with colorful veggies and three cheeses, then drenched with an egg custard, makes a rich, cheesy treat to start your morning with.

1 tablespoon extra-virgin olive oil

1 tablespoon butter

1 onion, chopped

2 garlic cloves, minced

1½ cups baby spinach leaves

1 red bell pepper, chopped

1 large tomato, seeded and chopped

1 cup cubed ham

Nonstick cooking spray

5 eggs, beaten

1 cup milk

½ teaspoon salt

½ teaspoon dried thyme leaves

⅛ teaspoon freshly ground black pepper

6 slices French bread, cubed

1 cup shredded Cheddar cheese

½ cup shredded Swiss cheese

¼ cup grated Parmesan cheese

1. In a medium saucepan over medium heat, heat the olive oil and butter. Add the onion and garlic, and sauté, stirring, until tender, about 6 minutes.

2. Add the spinach and cook until wilted, about 5 minutes. Remove from the heat and add the bell pepper, tomato, and ham.

3. Line the slow cooker with heavy-duty foil and spray with the nonstick cooking spray.

continued

4. In a medium bowl, beat the eggs, milk, salt, thyme, and black pepper well.

5. In the slow cooker, layer half of the French bread. Top with half of the vegetable and ham mixture, and sprinkle with half of the Cheddar and Swiss cheeses. Repeat the layers.

6. Pour the egg mixture over everything, and sprinkle with the Parmesan cheese.

7. Cover and cook on low for 6 hours, or until the temperature registers 160°F on a food thermometer and the mixture is set.

8. Using the foil sling, remove from the slow cooker, and serve.

PER SERVING Calories: 1052; Total fat: 58g; Saturated fat: 29g; Cholesterol: 529mg; Carbohydrates: 78g; Fiber: 7g; Protein: 58g

SEASONAL SUBSTITUTION During the summer months, use summer squash, green beans, fresh corn cut off the cob, tomatillos, or zucchini in this versatile dish.

SUMMER SQUASH AND MUSHROOM STRATA

SERVES 2

You can choose your favorite vegetables for this delicious breakfast. Just be sure to use the same amounts, and cut the vegetables to about the same size so the dish cooks perfectly in the same amount of time.

1 onion, chopped

2 garlic cloves, minced

1½ cups sliced cremini mushrooms

1 red bell pepper, chopped

1 yellow summer squash, chopped

Nonstick cooking spray

6 slices French bread, cubed

1 cup shredded Cheddar cheese

1 cup shredded Swiss cheese

5 eggs, beaten

1 cup milk

1 tablespoon Dijon mustard

½ teaspoon salt

½ teaspoon dried basil leaves

⅛ teaspoon freshly ground black pepper

1. In a medium bowl, mix the onion, garlic, mushrooms, bell pepper, and squash.

2. Spray the slow cooker with the nonstick cooking spray.

3. In the slow cooker, layer the bread, vegetable mixture, and Cheddar and Swiss cheeses.

4. In a medium bowl, beat the eggs, milk, mustard, salt, basil, and pepper until combined.

5. Pour the egg mixture into the slow cooker.

6. Cover and cook on low for 6 hours, or until the temperature registers 160°F on a food thermometer.

7. Cut into squares and serve.

PER SERVING Calories: 1012; Total fat: 50g; Saturated fat: 27g; Cholesterol: 528mg; Carbohydrates: 80g; Fiber: 6g; Protein: 62g

PREP
20 MINUTES

COOK
10 MINUTES
ON THE
STOVE TOP
plus
7 HOURS
ON LOW

GLUTEN-FREE

SOY-FREE

NUT-FREE

SAUSAGE BREAKFAST RISOTTO

SERVES 2

Risotto can be a particularly delicious breakfast choice with its rich, creamy, very hearty wake-me-up qualities. Sausage and vegetables make this recipe even more colorful.

8 ounces pork sausage

1 onion, chopped

2 garlic cloves, minced

Nonstick cooking spray

1 cup sliced cremini mushrooms

1 cup Arborio rice

3 cups Chicken Stock (page 28)

½ cup milk

½ teaspoon salt

½ teaspoon dried marjoram leaves

⅛ teaspoon freshly ground black pepper

⅓ cup grated Parmesan cheese

1 tablespoon butter

1. In a medium saucepan over medium heat, cook the sausage, onion, and garlic until the sausage is browned, about 10 minutes, stirring to break up the meat. Drain well.

2. Spray the slow cooker with the nonstick cooking spray.

3. In the slow cooker, combine the sausage mixture, mushrooms, and rice. Add the stock, milk, salt, marjoram, and pepper, and stir.

4. Cover and cook on low for 7 hours.

5. Stir in the cheese and butter. Let stand for 5 minutes, and then serve.

PER SERVING Calories: 907; Total fat: 44g; Saturated fat: 17g; Cholesterol: 126mg; Carbohydrates: 88g; Fiber: 4g; Protein: 38g

DID YOU KNOW? You can make this recipe with long-grain white rice, but the rice will be much softer. It can also be made with wild rice for a nice change of pace.

SAUSAGE QUICHE

PREP
20 MINUTES

COOK
15 MINUTES
ON THE
STOVE TOP
plus
6 HOURS
ON LOW

SERVES 2

Wake up to a piping hot quiche with a moist top crust, crumbly sausage, earthy mushrooms, and colorful bell pepper, all topped with melty cheese.

GLUTEN-FREE

SOY-FREE

NUT-FREE

8 ounces pork sausage

1 onion, chopped

1 cup sliced mushrooms

Nonstick baking spray containing flour

2 garlic cloves, minced

1 red bell pepper, chopped

1 cup shredded Cheddar cheese, divided

4 eggs, beaten

1 cup whole milk

½ cup all-purpose flour

½ teaspoon baking powder

½ teaspoon salt

½ teaspoon dried basil leaves

⅛ teaspoon freshly ground black pepper

⅓ cup grated Parmesan cheese

1. In a medium saucepan over medium heat, cook the sausage with the onions, stirring to break up the meat, until the sausage is browned, about 10 minutes. Drain well and add the mushrooms; cook, stirring, until the mushrooms give up their liquid and the liquid evaporates, about 5 minutes.

2. Line the slow cooker with heavy-duty foil. Spray the foil with the non-stick baking spray containing flour.

3. In the slow cooker, layer the sausage mixture, garlic, and bell pepper. Top with ½ cup of Cheddar cheese.

4. In a medium bowl, beat the eggs, milk, flour, baking powder, salt, basil, and pepper. Pour the egg mixture into the slow cooker and top with the remaining ½ cup of Cheddar cheese. Sprinkle with the Parmesan cheese.

5. Cover and cook on low for 6 hours, or until the quiche registers 160°F on a food thermometer, the edges are browned, and the center is set.

6. Remove from the slow cooker and let stand for 5 minutes; cut into wedges and serve.

PER SERVING Calories: 1024; Total fat: 67g; Saturated fat: 29g; Cholesterol: 504mg; Carbohydrates: 43g; Fiber: 4g; Protein: 61g

PREP
15 MINUTES

COOK
6 HOURS
ON LOW

SOY-FREE

BANANA BREAD CASSEROLE

SERVES 2

Banana bread makes a great casserole or strata when combined with French bread, bananas, and bacon. This is a fun casserole to make for a weekend morning. All you need to serve with it is orange juice and coffee.

Nonstick cooking spray

6 slices banana bread, cubed

6 slices French bread, cubed

1 banana, sliced

4 slices bacon, cooked and crumbled

½ cup chopped pecans

4 eggs, beaten

1½ cups milk

⅓ cup sugar

2 tablespoons honey

1 teaspoon ground cinnamon

1 teaspoon vanilla

¼ teaspoon salt

1. Spray the slow cooker with the nonstick cooking spray.

2. In the slow cooker, layer the banana bread, French bread, banana, bacon, and pecans.

3. In a medium bowl, beat the eggs, milk, sugar, honey, cinnamon, vanilla, and salt. Pour the egg mixture into the slow cooker.

4. Cover and cook on low for 6 hours, or until the temperature registers 160°F on a food thermometer, and serve.

PER SERVING Calories: 1392; Total fat: 54g; Saturated fat: 16g; Cholesterol: 444mg; Carbohydrates: 183g; Fiber: 7g; Protein: 50g

PREP IT RIGHT Banana bread can be made from a mix or from scratch, or it can be purchased at the store in the bakery department. For a casserole with a bit more crunch, toast the banana bread and French bread, cool, and then cut into cubes before you add them to the slow cooker.

PREP
15 MINUTES

COOK
6 HOURS
ON LOW

SOY-FREE

NUT-FREE

VEGETARIAN

CHOCOLATE–CHERRY-STUFFED FRENCH TOAST

SERVES 2

Slow cooker French toast has the texture of a strata, but the edges should be golden brown and crusty. This recipe kicks the taste up a notch with sweet cherries and chocolate.

Nonstick cooking spray

8 slices French bread

¾ cup mascarpone cheese

½ cup cherry preserves

¾ cup semisweet chocolate chips, melted

1 cup sliced pitted fresh cherries

5 eggs, beaten

1 cup milk

1 teaspoon vanilla

½ teaspoon ground cinnamon

¼ teaspoon salt

1. Line the slow cooker with heavy-duty foil, and spray with the nonstick cooking spray.

2. Spread one side of each slice of bread with the mascarpone cheese and the cherry preserves. Drizzle with the melted chocolate.

3. Cut the bread slices in half and layer them in the slow cooker with the fresh cherries.

4. In a medium bowl, beat the eggs, milk, vanilla, cinnamon, and salt. Pour the egg mixture into the slow cooker.

5. Cover and cook on low for 6 hours, or until the mixture is set and registers 160°F on a food thermometer. Remove from the slow cooker using the foil, slice, and serve.

PER SERVING Calories: 1447; Total fat: 53g; Saturated fat: 28g; Cholesterol: 467mg; Carbohydrates: 202g; Fiber: 10g; Protein: 45g

NEXT DAY This casserole can be warmed in the microwave for breakfast the next day, or bake it in a 400°F oven for about 10 minutes. You could also fry it in butter for a decadent treat.

PREP
15 MINUTES

COOK
5 MINUTES
ON THE
STOVE TOP
plus
6 HOURS
ON LOW

SOY-FREE

VEGETARIAN

PEACH FRENCH TOAST BAKE

SERVES 2

This rich, delicious dish with peaches and cream flavors is the perfect breakfast to wake up to. Serve with pineapple juice, hot coffee, and bacon or little sausages.

Nonstick cooking spray

½ cup brown sugar

3 tablespoons butter

1 tablespoon water

1 teaspoon vanilla

8 slices French bread

1½ cups peeled sliced peaches

4 eggs

1 cup milk

¼ cup granulated sugar

½ teaspoon ground cinnamon

¼ teaspoon salt

⅔ cup chopped pecans

1. Line the slow cooker with heavy-duty foil, and spray with the nonstick cooking spray.

2. In a small saucepan over low heat, bring the brown sugar, butter, and water to a simmer. Simmer about 5 minutes, stirring, until the mixture forms a syrup. Remove from the heat and stir in the vanilla.

3. In the slow cooker, layer in the bread and the peaches, drizzling each layer with some of the brown sugar syrup.

4. In a medium bowl, beat the eggs, milk, granulated sugar, cinnamon, and salt. Pour the egg mixture into the slow cooker and sprinkle with the pecans.

5. Cover and cook on low for 6 hours, or until the temperature registers 160°F on a food thermometer and the mixture is set.

6. Remove from the slow cooker, slice, and serve.

PER SERVING Calories: 1118; Total fat: 42g; Saturated fat: 17g; Cholesterol: 383mg; Carbohydrates: 158g; Fiber: 7g; Protein: 32g

SEASONAL SUBSTITUTION Fresh peaches are wonderful with this recipe, but you can use canned peaches if fresh are out of season. Make sure to buy peaches in light syrup, not heavy syrup, because the latter are too sweet for this recipe.

ELEVEN

DESSERTS

Cobblers, puddings, streusels, and crisps are naturals for slow cookers—stuffed apples, too. But did you know you can cook cake and cheesecake in this appliance? For a few of these recipes, you'll need a small specialty pan that fits inside your slow cooker, but once you have that, the sky is the limit. Enjoy these sweet recipes for the perfect end to your delicious meal.

APPLE-PEAR SAUCE

MAKES 8 CUPS

There's no easier recipe to make in the slow cooker than applesauce. This recipe freezes well, too: Cook the sauce and pack it into rigid freezer containers, leaving an inch of headspace. Label, seal, and freeze for up to 3 months.

Nonstick cooking spray

4 apples, peeled and sliced

3 firm pears, peeled and sliced

¼ cup apple cider

½ cup granulated sugar

2 tablespoons freshly squeezed lemon juice

1 teaspoon ground cinnamon

1 teaspoon ground nutmeg

⅛ teaspoon salt

1 teaspoon vanilla

1. Spray the slow cooker with the nonstick cooking spray.

2. In the slow cooker, combine the apples and pears, and stir.

3. Add the apple cider, sugar, lemon juice, cinnamon, nutmeg, and salt, and mix.

4. Cover and cook on low for 7 to 8 hours, or until the fruit is very soft.

5. Using a fork or potato masher, mash the mixture to the desired consistency. Stir in the vanilla and remove from the slow cooker.

6. Serve immediately or cool and then refrigerate for up to 4 days or freeze.

PER SERVING (1 cup) Calories: 148; Total fat: 1g; Saturated fat: 0g; Cholesterol: 0mg; Carbohydrates: 38g; Fiber: 5g; Protein: 1g

DID YOU KNOW? The apples you choose for this recipe should be good for cooking. They include Honey Crisp, Gala, Fuji, Granny Smith, Braeburn, Cortland, McIntosh, and Rome.

PREP
20 MINUTES

COOK
4 HOURS
ON LOW

SOY-FREE

VEGETARIAN

APPLE COBBLER

SERVES 2

In the world of desserts, cobblers and crisps are close cousins. A cobbler has a dough or biscuit-type topping, while a crisp uses a streusel. This cobbler is delicious served with a dollop of softly whipped cream.

Nonstick cooking spray

3 apples, peeled and sliced

1 tablespoon freshly squeezed lemon juice

½ cup dried cranberries

½ cup chopped walnuts

¼ cup granulated sugar, plus ⅓ cup, divided

⅔ cup all-purpose flour

½ teaspoon baking powder

1 egg, beaten

⅔ cup milk

1 teaspoon vanilla

1. Spray the slow cooker with the nonstick cooking spray.

2. Place the apples in the slow cooker, sprinkle with the lemon juice, and toss. Add the cranberries and walnuts, sprinkle with ¼ cup of granulated sugar, and toss again.

3. In a medium bowl, stir the flour, the remaining ⅓ cup of granulated sugar, the baking powder, egg, milk, and vanilla until smooth. Spoon the mixture over the apples in the slow cooker.

4. Cover and cook on low for 4 hours, or until the topping is set.

5. Serve warm with cream or ice cream.

PER SERVING Calories: 703; Total fat: 24g; Saturated fat: 3g; Cholesterol: 89mg; Carbohydrates: 110g; Fiber: 11g; Protein: 19g

APPLE-PEAR STREUSEL

PREP
20 MINUTES

COOK
7 HOURS
ON LOW

SOY-FREE

VEGETARIAN

SERVES 2

Although streusel topping gets crisp in the oven, in the slow cooker it's softer and creamier—but no less tantalizing. In this recipe, apple and pear come together with cinnamon and pecans to create an orchard-fresh experience.

Nonstick cooking spray

4 apples, peeled and sliced

2 pears, peeled and sliced

¼ cup brown sugar

1 tablespoon freshly squeezed lemon juice

½ teaspoon ground cinnamon

2 tablespoons butter, plus 3 tablespoons cut into cubes, divided

½ cup light cream

1 cup all-purpose flour

½ cup rolled oats

½ cup chopped pecans

⅓ cup granulated sugar

1. Spray the slow cooker with the nonstick cooking spray.

2. In the slow cooker, combine the apple and pear slices; sprinkle with the brown sugar, lemon juice, and cinnamon, and mix. Dot with 2 tablespoons of butter and pour the cream over everything.

3. In a medium bowl, combine the flour, oats, pecans, and granulated sugar. Add the remaining 3 tablespoons of butter cubes, and cut in with two knives or a pastry blender until crumbly. Sprinkle the mixture over the fruit.

4. Cover and cook on low for 7 hours, or until the fruit is tender.

PER SERVING Calories: 1112; Total fat: 34g; Saturated fat: 15g; Cholesterol: 64mg; Carbohydrates: 201g; Fiber: 21g; Protein: 13g

PREP IT RIGHT The best pears for cooking include Bosc with their brown skin, and Anjou, which have a pale green skin. Peel pears using a swivel-bladed peeler, then cut in half and cut out the core and stem. Slice pears crosswise for best results.

PREP
15 MINUTES

COOK
7 HOURS
ON LOW

SOY-FREE

NUT-FREE

VEGETARIAN

PUMPKIN PIE CUSTARD

SERVES 2

If you love pumpkin pie any time of the year but don't want to spend time making crust and filling and then baking, this pudding is for you. You can top each serving with a crumbled sugar cookie to mimic the crust.

Nonstick cooking spray

1½ cups light cream

1 (15-ounce) can solid-pack pumpkin

½ cup brown sugar

¼ cup granulated sugar

2 eggs, beaten

3 tablespoons melted butter

2 teaspoons vanilla

⅓ cup all-purpose flour

½ teaspoon baking powder

1 teaspoon ground cinnamon

¼ teaspoon ground nutmeg

¼ teaspoon ground allspice

3 large sugar cookies

Whipped cream, for garnish

1. Spray the slow cooker with the nonstick cooking spray.

2. In a large bowl, gradually add the light cream to the pumpkin, beating with a hand mixer.

3. Beat in the brown sugar, granulated sugar, eggs, butter, and vanilla.

4. Add the flour, baking powder, cinnamon, nutmeg, and allspice.

5. Pour the mixture into the slow cooker. Cover and cook on low for 7 hours, or until the mixture is set.

6. Crumble the sugar cookies on top of each serving, and serve with whipped cream.

PER SERVING Calories: 1216; Total fat: 68g; Saturated fat: 39g; Cholesterol: 332mg; Carbohydrates: 143g; Fiber: 8g; Protein: 16g

PREP IT RIGHT Only use solid-pack pumpkin, which is cooked pumpkin and nothing else, in this recipe. If you use pumpkin pie filling, which has sugar and other ingredients, the recipe will be too runny and too sweet.

LEMON RICE PUDDING

SERVES 2

The rice becomes very tender, and the lemon peel in this recipe cooks to a candy-like consistency. You don't need a thing with this dish; just enjoy.

Nonstick cooking spray

1 cup long-grain white rice

⅔ cup granulated sugar

4 cups milk

1 cup water

⅓ cup freshly squeezed lemon juice

2 teaspoons chopped lemon peel

Pinch salt

4 tablespoons butter, melted

1. Spray the slow cooker with the nonstick cooking spray.

2. In the slow cooker, combine all the ingredients and stir.

3. Cover and cook on low for 6 hours, or until the rice is very tender and the mixture has thickened, and serve.

PER SERVING Calories: 1070; Total fat: 34g; Saturated fat: 21g; Cholesterol: 101mg; Carbohydrates: 171g; Fiber: 2g; Protein: 23g

RICE PUDDING

PREP
10 MINUTES

COOK
5 HOURS
ON LOW

GLUTEN-FREE

SOY-FREE

VEGETARIAN

SERVES 2

Serve this simple pudding warm or cold. You can also use other fruits such as strawberries, cherries, or raspberries as a topping.

Nonstick cooking spray

1 cup short-grain white rice

5 cups milk

1 cup light cream

½ cup sugar

1 tablespoon butter

2 teaspoons vanilla

½ cup chopped mango

½ cup chopped peeled kiwi

1. Spray the slow cooker with the nonstick cooking spray.

2. In the slow cooker, combine all the ingredients except the mango and kiwi, and stir.

3. Cover and cook on low for 5 hours, or until the rice is tender and the pudding is thick. If you are home, stir it a few times while it's cooking.

4. Top with the mango and kiwi and serve.

PER SERVING Calories: 1120; Total fat: 38g; Saturated fat: 23g; Cholesterol: 132mg; Carbohydrates: 170g; Fiber: 2g; Protein: 28g

NEXT DAY Leftover rice pudding is excellent served cold. It will be quite thick, so you can add more milk or cream before serving if you'd like.

DOUBLE CHOCOLATE BREAD PUDDING

SERVES 2

This bread pudding is delicious, creamy, and full of chocolate. Serve it with ice cream, whipped cream, or hard sauce.

Nonstick cooking spray

6 cups cubed French bread

1 cup semisweet chocolate chips

2 cups chocolate milk

4 eggs, beaten

3 tablespoons butter, melted

½ cup brown sugar

¼ cup granulated sugar

3 tablespoons cocoa powder

2 teaspoons vanilla

1. Line the slow cooker with heavy-duty foil, and spray with the nonstick cooking spray.

2. In the slow cooker, combine the French bread and chocolate chips.

3. In a large bowl, beat all the remaining ingredients. Pour the mixture into the slow cooker.

4. Push the bread under the liquid. Let stand for 20 minutes.

5. Cover and cook on low for 3 hours, or until the mixture is set and reads 160°F on a food thermometer, and serve.

PER SERVING Calories: 1588; Total fat: 70g; Saturated fat: 40g; Cholesterol: 403mg; Carbohydrates: 218g; Fiber: 13g; Protein: 32g

PERFECT PAIR To make hard sauce, combine ¼ cup butter, at room temperature, with ¾ cup powdered sugar and 1 teaspoon vanilla. Beat until smooth. The sauce will melt into the warm bread pudding as you eat.

CARAMEL BREAD PUDDING

SERVES 2

PREP
15 MINUTES

COOK
5 MINUTES
ON THE
STOVE TOP
plus
7 HOURS
ON LOW

SOY-FREE

VEGETARIAN

This deeply satisfying bread pudding makes for a decadent and sticky-sweet dessert. It's best eaten warm right out of the slow cooker, but no one will judge you if you double the recipe and find yourself sneaking bites in the middle of the night.

Nonstick cooking spray

6 slices French bread, cubed

1 cup golden raisins

2 eggs, beaten

1¼ cups whole milk

⅓ cup granulated sugar

1 teaspoon vanilla

½ teaspoon ground cinnamon

⅛ teaspoon salt

⅓ cup brown sugar

2 tablespoons butter

1 tablespoon water

1. Spray the slow cooker with the nonstick cooking spray.

2. In the slow cooker, combine the bread cubes and raisins.

3. In a medium bowl, beat the eggs, milk, sugar, vanilla, cinnamon, and salt well. Pour the egg mixture into the slow cooker.

4. Cover and let stand for 10 minutes, occasionally pushing the bread down into the liquid.

5. Meanwhile, in a small saucepan over medium heat, simmer the brown sugar, butter, and water until a sauce forms, about 5 minutes. Drizzle over the bread in the slow cooker.

6. Cover and cook on low for 7 hours, or until the mixture is set, and serve.

PER SERVING Calories: 998; Total fat: 23g; Saturated fat: 12g; Cholesterol: 209mg; Carbohydrates: 182g; Fiber: 5g; Protein: 24g

PREP
15 MINUTES

COOK
5 MINUTES
ON THE
STOVE TOP
plus
3 HOURS
ON LOW

SOY-FREE

NUT-FREE

CHOCOLATE AND VANILLA CAKE

SERVES 2

This cake is so moist because it cooks in the slow cooker. Make sure the 8-by-4-inch loaf pan fits in your slow cooker before you begin. If it doesn't, use a pan that holds 6 cups. You'll need to be home for this recipe for safety reasons, since it requires a paper towel between the cover and insert.

Nonstick baking spray containing flour

1 cup all-purpose flour

⅓ cup granulated sugar

⅓ cup brown sugar

1 teaspoon baking powder

½ teaspoon baking soda

Pinch salt

¼ cup cocoa powder

¼ cup semisweet chocolate chips, finely chopped

3 tablespoons butter

¼ cup boiling water

½ cup light cream

1 egg

2 teaspoons vanilla

1. Spray an 8-by-4-inch loaf pan with the nonstick baking spray containing flour.

2. In a medium bowl, mix the flour, granulated sugar, brown sugar, baking powder, baking soda, and salt.

3. In a small saucepan over low heat, heat the cocoa powder, chocolate chips, butter, and water, stirring frequently, until the chocolate chips melt, about 5 minutes.

4. Add the cocoa mixture to the flour mixture. Add the cream, egg, and vanilla, and beat for 1 minute.

5. Pour the mixture into the loaf pan.

6. Place the loaf pan in the slow cooker, and pour ½ cup of water around the pan. Place a double layer of paper towels on top of the slow cooker, and add the cover.

7. Cook on low for 3 hours, or until the cake springs back when lightly touched with a finger.

8. Remove the pan from the slow cooker and cool for 5 minutes; invert onto a cooling rack, cool completely, and serve.

PER SERVING Calories: 915; Total fat: 39g; Saturated fat: 23g; Cholesterol: 161mg; Carbohydrates: 137g; Fiber: 7g; Protein: 12g

CHOCOLATE-CHERRY LAVA CAKE

SERVES 2

This delectable lava cake has a very moist, almost pudding-like interior. Combining the rich, gooey chocolate with tangy cherries, it truly is the perfect dessert for chocolate lovers.

Nonstick cooking spray

1 cup all-purpose flour

½ cup brown sugar

½ cup granulated sugar

¼ cup cocoa powder

1½ teaspoons baking powder

Pinch salt

½ cup chocolate milk

2 tablespoons melted butter

1 teaspoon vanilla

½ cup cherry preserves

3 tablespoons honey

1 cup boiling water

1. Spray the slow cooker with the nonstick cooking spray.

2. In the slow cooker, combine the flour, brown sugar, granulated sugar, cocoa powder, baking powder, and salt.

3. Whisk in the chocolate milk, butter, and vanilla.

4. Drop the cherry preserves by small spoonfuls over the batter.

5. Drizzle with the honey, and pour the boiling water over everything. Do not stir.

6. Cover and cook on low for 5 hours, or until the cake looks done (toothpick tests will not work since there is a layer of sauce on the bottom). Scoop out of the slow cooker to serve.

PER SERVING Calories: 1061; Total fat: 16g; Saturated fat: 10g; Cholesterol: 38mg; Carbohydrates: 229g; Fiber: 6g; Protein: 11g

PREP IT RIGHT You could use other preserves in this easy recipe. Apricot preserves would be delicious, as would orange marmalade. Just make sure you drop the preserves by small spoonfuls onto the cake; otherwise, they could burn on the bottom.

APRICOT CHEESECAKE

SERVES 2

PREP
20 MINUTES

COOK
4 HOURS
ON LOW
plus
5 MINUTES
ON THE
STOVE TOP

SOY-FREE

NUT-FREE

VEGETARIAN

Sweet graham crackers and delicate apricots elevate the flavors of this creamy, lush cheesecake. You'll need a 4-by-3-inch springform pan for this recipe. They can be found at baking supply stores or online.

Nonstick cooking spray

⅓ cup graham cracker crumbs

1 tablespoon melted butter

8 ounces cream cheese, at room temperature

2 teaspoons cornstarch

⅓ cup granulated sugar

Pinch salt

1 egg

¼ cup mascarpone cheese

1 cup canned sliced apricots, drained, divided

½ cup water

2 tablespoons honey

1 tablespoon orange juice

1. Spray a 4-inch springform pan with the nonstick cooking spray.

2. In a small bowl, combine the graham cracker crumbs and butter and mix well. Press the mixture into the bottom of the pan.

3. In a medium bowl, beat the cream cheese until smooth.

4. Add the cornstarch, sugar, salt, and egg, and beat until smooth. Beat in the mascarpone cheese.

5. Chop the apricots, and stir ⅓ cup into the cream cheese mixture.

6. Spoon the cream cheese mixture on top of the crust in the springform pan.

continued

7. Place a small rack in the slow cooker and add the water. Place the springform pan on the rack.

8. Cover and cook on low for 4 hours. Remove the pan from the slow cooker and cool for 1 hour.

9. In a small pan over low heat, bring the remaining ⅔ cup chopped apricots and the honey and orange juice to a simmer. Simmer for 5 minutes, until thickened. Spoon the mixture over the cheesecake, and then chill until cold, about 3 to 4 hours, and serve.

PER SERVING Calories: 854; Total fat: 54g; Saturated fat: 32g; Cholesterol: 238mg; Carbohydrates: 82g; Fiber: 3g; Protein: 17g

CHERRY-STUFFED APPLES

SERVES 2

Stuffed apples become very tender, and the bottoms almost caramelize in the slow cooker. Serve with cold cream drizzled over each warm serving for a delicious contrast.

3 apples

1 tablespoon freshly squeezed lemon juice

⅓ cup dried cherries

2 tablespoons apple cider

2 tablespoons honey

¼ cup water

1. Cut about half an inch off the top of each of the apples, and peel a small strip of the skin away around the top.

2. Using a small serrated spoon or melon baller, core the apples, making sure not to go through the bottom. Drizzle with the lemon juice.

3. Fill the apples with the dried cherries. Carefully spoon the cider and honey into the apples.

4. Place the apples in the slow cooker. Pour the water around the apples.

5. Cover and cook on low for 4 hours, or until the apples are soft, and serve.

PER SERVING Calories: 320; Total fat: 1g; Saturated fat: 0g; Cholesterol: 0mg; Carbohydrates: 82g; Fiber: 14g; Protein: 2g

DID YOU KNOW? You can make this recipe with any dried fruit. Golden raisins, dark raisins, dried cranberries, or chopped dried apricots or dates would all be delicious.

APPLE GRANOLA CRISP

PREP
15 MINUTES

COOK
6 HOURS
ON LOW

SOY-FREE

VEGETARIAN

SERVES 2

Using granola makes the topping on this delicious dessert a bit crisper (though the moist heat means it can't be as crisp as an oven-baked one). The bitterness of the cranberries is tamed by the crisp apples, sugar, and a splash of lemon juice.

Nonstick cooking spray

5 apples, sliced

⅓ cup dried cranberries

1 tablespoon freshly squeezed lemon juice

3 tablespoons brown sugar

⅔ cup all-purpose flour

⅓ cup granulated sugar

⅓ cup butter, cut into pieces

1 cup Granola (page 216)

1. Spray the slow cooker with the nonstick cooking spray.

2. In the slow cooker, combine the apples, cranberries, lemon juice, and brown sugar.

3. In a medium bowl, mix the flour and sugar. Add the butter and cut in with a pastry blender or two knives until pea-size pieces form. Stir in the granola.

4. Sprinkle the flour mixture over the apples.

5. Cover and cook on low for 6 hours, or until the apples are tender, and serve.

PER SERVING Calories: 1055; Total fat: 66g; Saturated fat: 27g; Cholesterol: 92mg; Carbohydrates: 215g; Fiber: 24g; Protein: 25g

Appendix A

1. The best way to make sure it's easy to clean your slow cooker is to use nonstick cooking spray or line the slow cooker with foil or a slow cooker bag. There may still be spots of food, even if you use a liner, but cleanup will be much easier.

2. Always turn off and unplug the slow cooker when you're done using it.

3. Make sure that the slow cooker insert is completely cooled before you try to clean it.

4. Never add cold water to a hot slow cooker insert, or it may crack.

5. Place the cooled slow cooker insert in the sink and add some dish soap. Add warm water and let it soak for an hour or two. Then scrub with a plastic scrubbie or plastic brush.

6. Never use a metal scouring pad on the slow cooker liner; it may scratch. Scratches will turn into cracks, which may hold bacteria that could make your food unsafe to eat.

7. If you need to clean the steel surround, use a cleaner made for glass stove tops. It won't scratch the surface and will clean the surround easily.

8. Many slow cooker inserts can be cleaned in the dishwasher. Read the instructions to make sure. Plastic lids may not be safe in the dishwasher.

9. You can remove the food from the slow cooker, fill it with warm water, then cover and cook on low for another hour or so to remove really stubborn food or food that is burnt onto the liner. Make sure that the water covers all the stuck-on food.

10. To deep clean your slow cooker, remove all traces of food. Fill it almost to the top with water, and then add about $\frac{1}{2}$ cup of plain vinegar. Add 1 tablespoon of baking soda and stir. Cover and cook on low for 3 to 4 hours. Then turn off the slow cooker, let it cool for an hour, remove the liner, and wash in the sink as you normally would.

THE CLEAN FIFTEEN & THE DIRTY DOZEN

A nonprofit environmental watchdog organization called Environmental Working Group (EWG) looks at data supplied by the U.S. Department of Agriculture (USDA) and the Food and Drug Administration (FDA) about pesticide residues. Each year it compiles a list of the best and worst pesticide loads found in commercial crops. You can use these lists to decide which fruits and vegetables to buy organic to minimize your exposure to pesticides and which produce is considered safe enough to buy conventionally. This does not mean they are pesticide-free, though, so wash these fruits and vegetables thoroughly.

These lists change every year, so make sure you look up the most recent one before you fill your shopping cart. You'll find the most recent lists as well as a guide to pesticides in produce at EWG.org/FoodNews.

2015 Dirty Dozen

Apples
Celery
Cherry tomatoes
Cucumbers
Grapes
Nectarines (imported)
Peaches
Potatoes
Snap peas (imported)
Spinach
Strawberries
Sweet bell peppers

In addition to the Dirty Dozen, the EWG added two types of produce contaminated with highly toxic organophosphate insecticides:

Kale/collard greens
Hot peppers

2015 Clean Fifteen

Asparagus
Avocados
Cabbage
Cantaloupes (domestic)
Cauliflower
Eggplants
Grapefruits

Kiwis
Mangoes
Onions
Papayas
Pineapples
Sweet corn
Sweet peas (frozen)
Sweet potatoes

Appendix C

MEASUREMENT CONVERSIONS

VOLUME EQUIVALENTS (LIQUID)

U.S. STANDARD	U.S. STANDARD (OUNCES)	METRIC (APPROXIMATE)
2 tablespoons	1 fl. oz.	30 mL
¼ cup	2 fl. oz.	60 mL
½ cup	4 fl. oz.	120 mL
1 cup	8 fl. oz.	240 mL
1½ cups	12 fl. oz.	355 mL
2 cups or 1 pint	16 fl. oz.	475 mL
4 cups or 1 quart	32 fl. oz.	1 L
1 gallon	128 fl. oz.	4 L

OVEN TEMPERATURES

FAHRENHEIT (F)	CELSIUS (C) (APPROXIMATE)
250°	120°
300°	150°
325°	165°
350°	180°
375°	190°
400°	200°
425°	220°
450°	230°

VOLUME EQUIVALENTS (DRY)

U.S. STANDARD	METRIC (APPROXIMATE)
⅛ teaspoon	0.5 mL
¼ teaspoon	1 mL
½ teaspoon	2 mL
¾ teaspoon	4 mL
1 teaspoon	5 mL
1 tablespoon	15 mL
¼ cup	59 mL
⅓ cup	79 mL
½ cup	118 mL
⅔ cup	156 mL
¾ cup	177 mL
1 cup	235 mL
2 cups or 1 pint	475 mL
3 cups	700 mL
4 cups or 1 quart	1 L

WEIGHT EQUIVALENTS

U.S. STANDARD	METRIC (APPROXIMATE)
½ ounce	15 g
1 ounce	30 g
2 ounces	60 g
4 ounces	115 g
8 ounces	225 g
12 ounces	340 g
16 ounces or 1 pound	455 g

Recipe Index

Index

CPSIA information can be obtained
at www.ICGtesting.com
Printed in the USA
BVHW02s1533131217
502716BV00015B/109/P